David Hunn

Gillian Gilks

A Life of Badminton

Ward Lock Limited · London

Acknowledgments

The author and publishers would like to thank the following for kindly supplying the photographs: Nick Skinner of Cassidy and Leigh, frontispiece; Central Press Photos, page 13 below; *Croydon Advertiser*, page 14 top; *The Scotsman*, page 29 below; Louis Ross, pages 30, 59, 63, 75, 76, 82, 91, 92, 103, 104, 113, 114, 115, 123, 124, 131, 132, 135, 136; *Sussex Life*, page 51; All-Sport/Tony Duffy, pages 60 and 81; Caters Photographic, page 64.
The jacket design and front photograph are by Behram Kapadia.
The back jacket photograph is by Mike Webster.

First published in Great Britain in 1981
by Ward Lock Limited, 47 Marylebone Lane,
London W1M 6AX, a Pentos Company.

House editor Gillian Freeman

Text set in Times
by Computacomp (UK) Ltd
Fort William, Scotland

Printed in Great Britain by Butler and Tanner Ltd
Frome and London

British Library Cataloguing in Publication Data
Hunn, David
Gillian Gilks: A Life of Badminton
1. Badminton (Game) players –
Biography
I. Title
796.34'5 GV1007

ISBN 0-7063-6114-8

Contents

Foreword 5

1 Take two geese ... 7

2 Girl with a secret 11

3 Full speed ahead 16

4 Cape Town to Tokyo 21

5 A bundle of fire 26

6 Hot air and other hazards 37

7 Gold and more gold 44

8 Disaster and discontent 56

9 Break with Beck 68

10 Superwoman 78

11 Double trouble 86

12 Outbreak of hostilities 97

13 Money and more money 107

14 Cutting loose 121

15 The best of British 130

Addendum: Badminton champions 1965–1980 140

Gillian Gilks, MBE, in 1976: triple champion of Europe, the Commonwealth and All-England

Foreword

During the summer of 1980, Gillian Gilks was visited by the most extraordinary transformation. It arrived by invitation, at the hands of a plastic surgeon. The famous Gilks nose, that had faced demoralised badminton victims in every continent of the world, was banished in favour of a more delicate and delightful frontispiece. Shortly afterwards, Mrs Gilks found herself a new hairstyle to match. Two styles, in fact: the first, pictured on the back of the jacket of this book, proved more attractive than convenient for a badminton player, and its loose tresses had to be confined by a head-band; the second, a confection of tight and tumbling curls, seemed admirable. A new woman was created.

It is difficult to appreciate how startling it was, for someone who had known the lady for several years, to walk into the room one day and find another person sitting in her chair — a person who, it was soon clear, was not only more smashing to behold but who had become a brighter and more confident person. On court, the fantastic legs and the unique style were as unmistakeable as ever, but when she was sitting nearby, even some of her fellow-players did not recognise her.

Action as drastic as that, particularly with the gamble involved, must be strongly motivated. Gillian admits her reasons were largely psychological. She had become undeniably self-conscious — almost certainly unnecessarily so — about the prominence of her nose in what is, or used to appear to be, a face ruled by bone. In the street, she thought she could feel the eyes of the public drawn to her nose; on court, with her long, straight blonde hair drawn tightly back, she left them little else to look at.

She first contemplated such an operation soon after her marriage; but with the ending of that relationship in 1976, neither money nor time was easy to find. As the years passed and her badminton worries increased, so did her need for self-confidence. Today, she holds her head happily high again. She has been able to face up to the seemingly interminable confrontations with the Badminton Association of England, despite the depressing effects of that obstinate battle over the rights of the individual. For championing those rights, badminton players will one day bless Gillian Gilks, though some of them have been reluctant to associate too closely with her during the period of hostilities. Whatever the immediate result may be of the litigation between Gilks and the BAE, everybody knows where badminton is going: it is moving — with determination on the part of the players, with reluctance on the part of the governing bodies — towards money-spinning badminton circuits. Who organises them on the players' behalf will probably depend on who first becomes fully aware of the potential involved and sets their house in order accordingly. Meanwhile, like Jonah Barrington in squash and Tony Greig in cricket, Gillian has gone out in front and carried the colours, parried the bullets.

To those who have made it possible for me to put this book together, some slabs of gratitude are due. To the editors of *The Times*, *The Guardian* and *The Daily Telegraph*, who were covering badminton regularly long before it was fashionable to do so; to *The Observer*, for allowing me to quote from some of my own work for that paper; to the *Badminton Gazette*, from whose faithful coverage I have often drawn; to Louis Ross, the photographer whose dedication to the sport in the past seven years has provided a unique pictorial record; and particularly to Gillian's mother, Mrs Perrin, who has meticulously preserved a factual account of her daughter's life in badminton for the past twenty years.

Yapton, Sussex
February, 1981

I Take two geese . . .

It is quite hard to take seriously a game that can only be played by sticking sixteen white goose feathers into a piece of cork. And not any old goose feathers: the bird only produces eight on each wing that are suitable for the job, and even that does not lead to the convenient equation that one goose equals one shuttle. All the feathers on the shuttle must come from the same side of the bird, so it takes two right wings to make a shuttle, and two left wings to make another one. Can we be talking about the most popular participant sport in Britain, or is this Alice in Wonderland?

As the world's leading manufacturers, Reinforced Shuttlecocks Limited, admit to marketing 'many hundreds of thousands of dozens' of shuttles every year, you could be forgiven for imagining that the world's white geese spend a good deal of time looking anxiously over their shoulders for the approach of a man with a pair of pincers. It doesn't happen. The man will be carrying a club, or whatever they kill geese with these days. The feathers RSL need are only a by-product of slaughter, so you can be pretty sure that nobody plucks a goose anywhere in the world without the man from RSL rushing round with a sack. The firm buys constantly from Poland, Czechoslovakia, Hungary, Italy, France — any place you hear a goose squawk, they'll be there. That's not the end of their importing problems: the cork comes from Spain and Portugal, the kid that covers it from Australia and New Zealand, the linen thread from Ireland. All that Britain can produce, it seems, is the glue that holds it together and the metal pellet that gives it weight — not that there's much of that, since the whole thing weighs only one-fifth of an ounce, which is precisely as much as a tablespoonful of corn flakes.

It's easy enough to see the point of this piece of nonsense. Whack it as hard as you like, by the time it has travelled half-way down the court it's on the way to standing still. You'll break no windows with a shuttlecock. You'll not even knock the Ming vase off the chimneypiece, as they discovered in the front hall of Badminton House more than a century ago. What puzzles the mind exceedingly, and defies research utterly, is who and why and when and where anyone should have done it in the first place. Even Bernard Adams, who in 1979 wrote the only scholarly history of the game, admits to being mystified. There was, of course, battledore and shuttlecock before badminton, but that explains nothing. In Ancient Greece and the Orient they have been batting shuttlecocks to and fro for two thousand years and more, and even in England for six hundred years. Strung rackets have been used outdoors since the 17th century, but even then the purpose of the game was purely the faintly amusing one of trying to keep the shuttle in the air for as long as possible — between two people, or even by one player holding two rackets. Even in Badminton House (home of the Somerset family now headed by the Duke of Beaufort) that patient pastime persisted to the middle of the 19th century. In 'The Badminton Story', Adams quotes the inscriptions on two of the parchment-covered battledores preserved there. On one: 'Kept up with Lady Somerset on Saturday January 12th 1830 to 2117' and on the other: 'The Lady Henrietta Somerset in February 1845 kept up with Beth Mitchell 2018.'

Though there appears to be no documentary evidence to support the claim, it is firmly believed by the Beauforts that battledore and shuttlecock was developed into 'badminton' in mid-century by the children of that great house putting a string across the hall from the front door to the fireplace and batting across it. Others ascribe the invention to adult house guests at Badminton, and by 1860 there was a booklet on sale in London entitled 'Badminton battledore — a new game'. The compilers of the Encyclopaedia Britannica seem convinced, as some others are, that the game was played in India before England. A delightful photograph exists, said to have been taken in India in 1867, showing a very well-organised game of badminton being played outdoors on a clearly-marked court. By the 1870s badminton had seized India firmly — or at least its British, white, expatriate population. The Bishop of Madras protested against Sunday badminton from his pulpit in February 1877, and *The Times of India* was moved to agree that in Calcutta too, morning badminton was played openly on Sundays: 'In Bombay we are more virtuous, if abstention be a virtue, for after all, leaving religious views aside, it is a matter chiefly of public decorum.' It was in India, too, that the weird 'hour-glass' shape of the court originated, a peculiarity that lasted until the 20th century. The sidelines were nipped in at the net, where the court was four feet narrower than at the baseline. The recess was sharp and V-shaped and had absolutely no purpose at all except to accommodate two doors that opened inwards in the centre of each side of the hall in which the game was played.

Rules are said to have been framed at Poona in 1873 and were published ten years later, at which time the game seems to have been played more frequently out of doors than indoors. That may have been acceptable in the predictable climate of India, but England's breezes ensured that the game did not develop beyond social entertainment until it became firmly established indoors towards the end of the century. Competitive badminton was launched with an open tournament at Guildford in 1898, and the first All-England championships were held in London the following year. It was a one-day event comprising only men's, women's and mixed doubles; singles being still regarded as a highly unsocial form of the game. The serious and successful exponents of badminton were then, and for some years remained, already accomplished tennis players; for though badminton was certainly established before lawn tennis (or sphairisticke, as its inventor first called it), tennis developed very much more rapidly in its early years. The editorial in the first issue of *The Badminton Gazette*, in November 1907 (by which time 220 clubs were affiliated to the Badminton Association) looked forward 'to the time, not far distant, when it will be as well known as Lawn Tennis.'

Herbert Scheele, in a programme note for the 1978 All-England, recalled some hilarious incidents (and some disappointing ones) during the history of those championships. The legendary Sir George Thomas arriving for his first championships in 1900, at the age of 18, to find the Association's honorary secretary on his hands and knees marking the lines on the floor in chalk; one (indoor) final being abandoned because of failing light; and the horrors of the first post-war championships in 1947. That tournament was held in Harringay Arena and was never to be forgotten. Few of us now over the age of fifty will fail to recall that awful winter, colder than any in our lives and one that coincided with the national fuel shortage. On the night before the championships opened, a severe blizzard hurled snow in through the air vents in the roof on to the five courts. Though this was swept away in the morning, the moisture that remained froze mercilessly — not only was there no heating in the hall, but the floor was laid on top of an ice rink. Only six of the scheduled sixty matches could be played on the first day. That was also the humiliating year in which England, for the first time, won not one title. British domination of the game was over and it never returned.

Sir George Thomas, who himself won four singles titles and seventeen men's and mixed doubles titles over a period of 25 years, was so appalled that he inaugurated the Thomas Cup for international men's teams, in the hope that it would spur England's men to greater effort. The effort may have been there, but success did not attend it: neither England nor any other European nation has ever won the trophy; nor the women's equivalent, the Uber Cup, founded in 1956; and it is now quite hard to believe that they ever will. The game has changed out of sight since Thomas's day. He won his last All-England singles title at 41, and at 46 he was still nimble enough to take the men's doubles. Today, an average All-England match will last 45 minutes, during the course of which each player will run a mile with 350 changes of direction of 90 degrees or more. The shuttle will actually be in flight for 20 of the 45 minutes (a tennis ball is only in play for eight per cent of the time a match takes) and it will be struck 400 times. No wonder RSL are kept busy!

This was the world into which little Gillian Perrin crept, a frail-looking child who had already astonished adults with the maturity of her badminton when, at the age of 14, she first played in the All-England senior championships. She became what everybody was sure she was going to become: the most outstanding British player, of either sex, since badminton became a truly international game. To this day, only four Britons have won an All-England singles title in the past 40 years, and only Gillian Gilks has won it twice. This book is the story of her extraordinary achievements and her highly controversial life in badminton — not necessarily the way she sees it, but the way I do. As it whips along that road, it becomes also, if only incidentally, the story of badminton in the past twenty years. And since it seems clear that at least a million schoolchildren play that game, and more than three million competitive club members, and who knows how many hundreds of thousands of us banging away in the back garden when the wind isn't too strong, there is no way anybody can pretend that story is not important. As for the geese, they can rest assured that most of us use plastic shuttles.

2 Girl with a secret

Gillian Gilks possesses a power of recollection of which many an elephant would be utterly ashamed. Let us consider November 23rd, 1966 — barely the day before yesterday in the calendar of life, and the day on which she learned she had become the youngest woman ever to be picked to play badminton for England. How? When? Where? The moment is surely etched in gold through her very soul; the words must even now glow within her mind.

'I don't really remember,' she said. 'Perhaps my father told me.' Let's say he did. He might well have done, picking her up in the afternoon at Nonsuch Grammar School, Cheam, Surrey, and taking her off for homework — or more likely badminton practice. And would he have had a call from the Badminton Association, or maybe discreetly opened an intriguing-looking letter? He might, but he didn't. He had a call from a friend who had read the *London Evening News*. Not for the first or last time, the secrets of selection had been leaked to the Press.

The official letter arrived two days later: 'I have pleasure in sending you this invitation to play for England v Scotland at Barnt Green, near Birmingham, on Thursday December 15th commencing at 7 p.m. Please be kind enough to notify me of your acceptance as soon as possible. Apologies are extended for the fact that news of the team selected should have appeared in the national Press before you received this invitation. It is not quite clear as to how it was obtained by the Press before being known in this office.'

The match against Scotland being one in which new talent is often blooded, the selection of the 16-year-old schoolgirl was not as astonishing as it might have been. But, despite her tournament successes, Gillian had only ten days earlier played for her county for the first time. Surrey were rich in badminton power, and could thrash all comers without calling on their infant prodigy. The girl had been a sensation ever since, at the age of nine, she first played a serious game of badminton. She was still at that ridiculous age when her father entered her for the Surrey Junior tournament, a perky blonde matchstick girl whose legs looked little thicker than the handle of her racket. With the encouraging handicap of plus-eight, she won a couple of sets and caused enough eye-boggling to persuade the family she must join the Wimbledon club as well as the Cheam. Wimbledon was one of the hot spots of the game. Cheam had one court with low ceiling, Wimbledon had four courts with perfect facilities, top players, top coaches.

At eleven, Gillian entered the All-England Junior Championships (under-18). She won no matches, no games and only one point, but responded to such treatment by winning the under-15 Surrey singles. The next year the All-England for the first time included an under-15 section. She won it then, despite having match point against her in the second game of the final, and she won it for the next two years. She began to scoop up all the cups Surrey could offer: the under-15 and the under-18 singles, the under-18 doubles — and still she was only twelve.

At 13, there was not a junior player in the country who could face her with absolute confidence and the badminton Press was beginning to hum. After the Northern Championships, the *Badminton Gazette* had this to say of her: 'Mention must be made of the quarter-final in which little Gillian Perrin of Surrey came on court for her third singles long after her normal bedtime, and after reaching match-point in the second game against Miss Bridge finally tired and lost 11–7, 11–12, 7–11. But what a lovely player she is, and with physical maturity she must surely become a great one.'

In the same issue 'Invicta' stuck his neck out a long way: 'The most outstanding player of the whole tournament, insofar as the future is concerned, was a little girl of $13\frac{1}{2}$ years by the name of Gillian Perrin. Quite a stripling still, it must be a secret where her power comes from. Certainly it is not muscularly apparent. She seems clearly an embryonic champion in senior ranks, and I have never seen any youngster of her merit at anything like her age. Not only has she the strokes and the necessary touch, but she also seemed to have an uncanny sense of general tactics.'

Domestically, her dominance was getting embarrassing. In 1964, still only 13, she took the under-15, under-18 and under-20 Surrey singles titles — still enjoying, of course, a handicap that took more favourable account of her age than of her ability. Nothing meant very much any more except that she should land the big one, the All-England Junior (under-18) title, which she duly did at the age of 14 — the youngest girl champion in history. 'Invicta' did his nut:

'To see her clear the shuttle from high up on the backhand to almost the full length of the court is a joy to behold, as is the really crisp way in which she strokes, rather than hits, the shuttle all the time.'

Three months later Gillian qualified for the first time for the All-England senior championships, both in singles and (with Janet Prince) in the women's doubles. No, at 14 the impossible could not possibly be done: she lost both first round matches emphatically, a habit she continued in the singles championship for an uncommon number of years. No doubt her morale was somewhat restored in the Surrey Junior, when she again won all three girls' singles, despite playing two from scratch and the under-15 off a handicap of minus-five.

By the time she was 16, Gillian had won the All-England under-15 singles title three times and the under-18 twice, and opponents of anything less than top class

(right) *The matchstick girl, aged 11, with Surrey colleagues Angela Bairstow* (left) *and Anthea Swinstead; and* (below) *two years later, already the All-England under-15 champion*

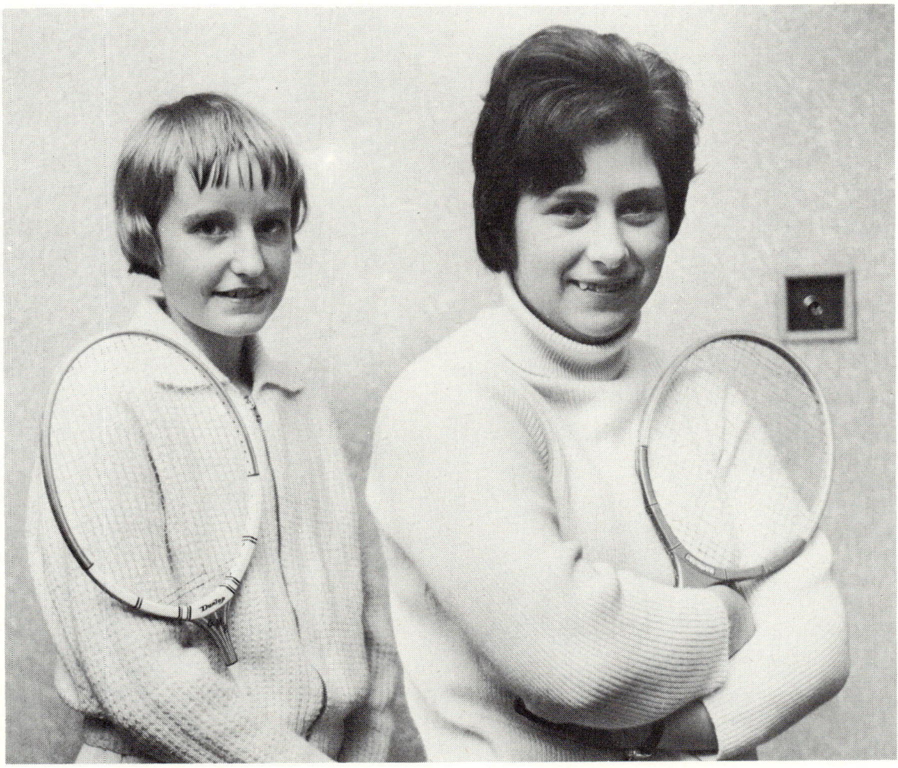

At 14, Gillian Perrin became the youngest girl ever to add the junior championship of All-England (under-18) to her trophies. In December 1966 (below) *the 16-year-old schoolgirl became the youngest badminton player to win an England 'cap'*

were beginning to look forward to winning points from her, not games. Perhaps fortunately, she was getting no badminton at school, which she was representing at tennis, hockey, netball and rounders. In the evenings and at weekends, badminton was her diet, and by now she was having to hold up her dish in the open, senior tournaments. It seldom came away empty.

In October 1966 the prodigious child took her place among the women. In the final of the West Sussex Open at Littlehampton, she beat her Surrey colleague, English international Julie Charles, 11–5, 11–1; two weeks later, in the Surrey Restricted, she made another Surrey international, Iris Rogers, come close to sweating blood before the senior player won 11–12, 11–7, 11–9; the next day Gillian and international Angela Bairstow won the women's doubles. Who could shut her out now? The county selectors certainly couldn't, picking her at last for both doubles in a match against Hampshire. And so to England, at seven p.m. on Thursday December 15th, 1966, aged $16\frac{1}{2}$ years.

It was the launching of an extraordinary international career, the first 'cap' of 68 spread over the next 14 years. Gillian Gilks, as she was later, became what the experts knew she would be: one of the greatest badminton players the world had ever seen. Where is her equal as an all-round player? Hiroe Yuki was the more consistent singles player and Lene Koppen may prove even better; Nora Perry would now get the vote as a doubles specialist. But Gillian Gilks, as well as winning the All-England singles title twice, won the women's doubles three times with three different partners and the mixed four times with two partners. Only the legendary Judy (Devlin) Hashman can beat that, with her ten singles and seven women's doubles titles and then, international competition was not what it is now.

The pattern of Mrs Gilks' triumphs was peculiar indeed. From being the youngest-ever winner of the junior All-England title, she became, eleven years later, one of the oldest players to take the senior title for the first time. It was then, at the summit of her glory, that life began to clip her round the ear. Her marriage broken, she developed an aggressive resistance to being messed about by the amateur rulers of her increasingly-professional game. She began to dig in her heels and heave back on the rope, and the other side responded by cutting her end of the rope adrift.

By careful administration of the prolonged dispute, the establishment figures were able to show her as being selfish, pig-headed and unpatriotic. In so doing, thanks to her stubborn refusal to concede, they exposed their own stupidity, which fluctuated from pathetic to pompous, with an occasional hint of real malice. It was the sort of sorry scene that amateur sport is adept at mounting, but it was more tragic than most. In the end, it deprived England of their greatest player, and the player of her proper opportunities. It was a game without a winner.

3 Full speed ahead

There was no great hurry for Gillian to hit her next target, but there was no doubt what the target was. Inevitably, the day was going to arrive when Angela Bairstow, the queen of British badminton, could no longer withstand the rapidly-growing challenge of the teenaged lady-in-waiting. It was an uncomfortable time for Miss Bairstow, the Empire Games and English national champion, who must have been heartily sick of reading that her young county colleague was the greatest prospect we had bred since Heather Ward, who won the All-England in 1959.

Both were coached at Wimbledon by one of the most dedicated and talented men in that game, Ian Palmer, whose expertise at spotting winners young was unrivalled. Palmer had a yacht at Itchenor. Gillian and her childhood badminton partner, Jane Colman, used to be taken sailing in Chichester Harbour from time to time. It was, Gillian recalls, a bit odd: sometimes they would go with Ian and Babs, his wife, and sometimes with Ian and Angela, who became his wife.

A very determined and aggressive player, Miss Bairstow was shorter but at the time a lot stronger than Gillian. During the 1966–67 season, in which the schoolgirl first played for England, it seemed to be Gillian's lot frequently to be drawn in the same half of open tournaments as Miss Bairstow, and to lose to her in the singles semi-finals. In February they met in the final of the Irish Open, and the writing began to appear on the wall. In the finest match she had ever played, Gillian took the first game 12–10 and lost the other two 8–11, 8–11. Though her England partner was Iris Rogers, the selectors began to encourage Gillian and Angela to play together (they were partners for Surrey), recognising that there lay there a potentially unbeatable pair. In the last tournament before the 1967 All-England, they took the Britannic Invitation title.

Once again the All-England had an early grave waiting for the eager child. She lost her first match to the Dutch woman, Felice de Nooyer, as well as her first mixed doubles with Jim Sydie. In the women's doubles there was better luck — and worse. She reached the semi-final with Mrs Rogers before her partner had to withdraw, with tonsilitis. Gillian went back to Wimbledon, highly peeved, won five titles (under-18 and under-20) in the Surrey Junior, and faced the summer and her seventeenth birthday with even more determination.

The first open tournament of the new season was a comparatively minor affair, the West Hampshire at Bournemouth. It was an unforgettable day, October 21st: Gillian won the mixed doubles with Roger Mills, the women's doubles with Angela Bairstow, and the singles. For the first time in her life, she beat the only woman who was consistently beating her. Miss Bairstow fell 6–11, 11–7, 6–11. Six days later they met again in the Surrey Restricted final. Miss Bairstow swept through the first set 11–3, Gillian levelled with 11–7 in the second. The third had all the Surrey players in a frenzy of excitement: leading by 10–6, the champion held six match points — and lost 12–10. For the future of English badminton, the most encouraging feature of the match was that both Gillian's strength and her nerve held in the most testing circumstances.

Gillian was not foolish enough to think that she had now disposed of Angela Bairstow. A week later they faced each other again, in the final of the Wimbledon Open (one of the happiest facts of her badminton life by then was that Gillian was frequently seeded second to Angela, and so had no chance of meeting her until the finals). Gillian lost that one conclusively enough, but with some splendid compensations: on the way she beat three English internationals — Margaret Boxall, Julie Charles and the former national champion Ursula Smith. In a way, this was the most comfortable time of her badminton life. Her days of purely junior competition were over, when she often 'froze' at the crucial moments; her days of top-level senior battle were yet to come. As a youngster in senior circles, little was expected of her; and consequently she was frequently able to play beyond her best.

There was obviously no question of infallibility approaching the 17-year-old, but nevertheless defeats were beginning to hurt just a little, particularly when they came unexpectedly. Picked for the first time to play the singles for England, against Ireland in November, Gillian lost to Mary Bryan. The very next day, in the Northern Open, she lost to her again; two weeks later she and Angela Bairstow lost their doubles against West Germany and the next week Gillian, seeded for the Lancashire Open singles, was put out in the first round by Sue Pound (who became better-known as Sue Whetnall). The English Nationals were the next major hurdle, and again she lost to Miss Bairstow. But again she beat Ursula Smith, reinforcing her position at least as England's number two.

Miss Smith fell to her again in the London Open at Crystal Palace, leading to yet another final with Miss Bairstow. This was one of the most important open tournaments of the year and in it Gillian Perrin took a giant step towards glory. She won the singles 12–9, 12–10 and then partnered Angela to a doubles victory. There had not been a day like it in her life. She soared through the All-England Junior in the New Year, crushing young Margaret Beck 11–1, 11–1 — and how many dozen times did they meet in the next ten years? Straightaway she was off to Malmo for the first foreign tournament for which she had been nominated, the Swedish Open. Anne Flindt, of Denmark, put her out of the singles instantly, but she and Roger Mills — a partnership that was to flourish mightily — got as far as the semi-finals.

By now Angela Bairstow had temporarily lost favour with the selectors, for reasons that are not clear but could not have been solely concerned with her playing skill (she once more beat Gillian in the Kent final). Ursula Smith was picked for the singles against Scotland (Gillian was taking 'A' levels) and Gillian returned against Denmark. She lost to Bente Sorensen, who a few days later found herself drawn against Gillian again in the first round of the 1968 All-England. By now the bogey of this, the most important of all international tournaments, was beginning to fuss the girl a bit, and it didn't help to face a woman who had just beaten her. Gillian was disastrously disappointing, going down 11–5, 11–1 and fighting, in the end, for breath as well as honour. Breathing had troubled her before, and it would again, usually when the mental and physical pressures were greatest.

As soon as the All-England was over, there was another international and another defeat for Gillian, this time at the hands of the brilliant Swedish champion, Eva Twedberg. It was the youngster's sixth international, and her third defeat in three matches as England's singles player. For the first European Championships, in West Germany in April, Margaret Boxall and Angela Bairstow played the singles; Gillian came back with two silver medals, losing with Angela to Miss Boxall and Sue Whetnall, and with Roger Mills to Tony Jordan and Sue Whetnall.

Despite the disappointments that march ever closer as ambition and talent stride forward, the 1967–68 season had been the most exciting and impressive one of her dazzling little life. The next one opened, predictably, with an invitation to join the Uber Cup squad, which it was hoped might in 1969 wrest the women's international team trophy from Japan in Tokyo. During the summer recess Gillian left school to take an advanced secretarial course at Ewell Technical College, and Angela Bairstow became Mrs Palmer. With her retirement as a competitive singles player, the English prizes began to fall between Gilks, Boxall and Whetnall, with little Maggie Beck edging closer to them.

Gillian set off at high speed. Before October was out, she had won the West Sussex and Wimbledon singles, and all three Surrey Restricted titles; and she had lost the London Open to Eva Twedberg in 19 minutes. In December she became the youngest holder of the English National crown (nobody but Ursula Smith and Angela Bairstow had got their hands on it before), beating Miss Beck 11–3, 11–1 in the final. In January she continued her unhappy record of singles play for England, which was fast becoming as dismal as her All-England history: against Sweden she lost to Miss Twedberg again, and against Denmark to Imre Nielsen. But then, in her nineteenth year, the sun really began to shine on Gillian Perrin.

In the Swedish Open, Margaret Boxall beat Miss Twedberg, and Gillian beat Miss Boxall and the Danish champion, Anne Flindt, to take the title. In the European semi-final of the Uber Cup they faced Denmark, who had won every match against England for the past 35 years. Gillian went out for the first match against Imre Nielsen, fell 3–9 down and won 12–9, 11–2. With Julie Charles as her partner, she won both her doubles, and England took the tie. The next day Gillian took the Kent singles title, against the South African champion Wilma Prade, and in partnership for the first time in her life with the veteran Judy Hashman, beat the brilliant Boxall-Whetnall team for the doubles title. In the next four weeks she won the Essex, Dutch, Irish and Surrey singles titles, beginning in the Dutch her famous mixed doubles partnership with Derek Talbot.

It was hardly surprising that during February she received a handwritten letter from the chairman of selectors, J. D. McColl, advising her to cut down her badminton. No more mid-week training, he suggested, fewer tournaments and fewer county games, and less mixed doubles. By then the selectors knew that, provided England beat West Germany in the European Zone final in Hamburg, their girls would in the summer be facing an exhausting tour to South Africa and Japan. The circular letter sent to the Uber Cup squad at the beginning of the season had made quite plain what the girls were facing — as well as making quite plain the harshly autocratic attitude taken by the amateur administrators of the Badminton Association of England towards their voluntary and unpaid players:

> 'Membership of the squad will involve obedience to the instructions of myself or nominee (from the selectors' committee), arduous training and practice, and sacrifice of time and probably some money, although we can defray most expenses. You will be required to report to me at regular intervals on your progress and results, and some of the less successful performers will be omitted as time proceeds. I hope you will agree to join us. It won't be easy as we shall require hard work all along the line, with singles as the basic training medium. If you are game, good show. If you can't dedicate yourself, turn the invitation down. Please reply to me at the above address. J. D. McColl.'

Four nights of badminton a week were rightly reckoned as insufficient training to develop the speed, strength and stamina that would be needed to beat the Japanese. The squad members were sent a circuit training and interval training schedule that today's players would regard as quaintly naive, but which at the time shook them up slightly. These were still fairly early days for amateur sportsmen, particularly in a non-contact sport, to be asked to build their bodies.

These five exercises had to be executed in the right order, as quickly as possible, and with absolutely no break between them:

1 Shuttle runs. Four lengths of the court, running sideways but never crossing the legs.

2 Press-ups. At least five, preferably 15. NB Not necessarily on floor; supported against stool, chair etc. will be in order.

3 Pike jumps. From standing, leap in the air and touch toes, legs straight. Ten jumps.

4 Burpees. From standing, to crouch position, shoot both legs backwards to front support position, return legs to crouch, stand up. Ten times.

5 Pull-ups. Using a table, bars, etc., or could be done by grasping hands of another person. Ten times.

A ten minute rest was then recommended, before the interval training.

Three lengths of the court
1 Running forwards.
2 Running backwards.
3 Running forwards.
Rest ten seconds, then repeat.

Judging by her results through the season, all that was doing Gillian a power of good. Of course, she couldn't win them all. In the European Uber Cup final, hers was the only game England did not win. Marie-Louise Wackerow beat her, 11–8, 11–2. And then there was the All-England again. 'Miss Perrin seemed listless, short of judgement and unable in any way to impress her game and personality on her opponent,' was the finding of *The Times*. It was another first round defeat, the fourth year in which she had won no singles at all. This time it was another Dutch player who killed her hopes, Lily ter Metz. There was disaster too in the doubles, in which she had teamed up with Heather (Ward) Nielsen. They lost immediately to the unseeded Japanese pair, ultimately finalists, Amano and Takahashi. Despite all that, it was England's best year at the All-England since Heather Ward's win. David Eddy and Robert Powell, quite astonishingly, reached the doubles final, Margaret Boxall and Sue Whetnall won the women's, and with Roger Mills, Gillian lost only one game in the entire championships. That was to a Danish pair in the semis; in the final they obliterated the former English champions, Tony Jordan and Sue Whetnall, by 15–5, 15–3.

Still only 18, that was the 58th senior title Gillian Perrin had won, a stupendous achievement. And as that season closed, Gillian could reflect that it had brought her and Roger Mills no fewer than eight mixed titles at the highest level — the All-England, the English National, and the Swedish, London, Surrey, Wimbledon, Essex and Bucks Opens. A ninth was the Dutch Open that she won with Derek Talbot, and she had won a good handful of women's doubles. As a mixed doubles player she had transformed herself into one of the world's greatest, but that would have been little compensation to her if she had failed as a singles player.

Failing at the final hurdle she certainly was, but there was time to correct that. It was quite unprecedented in the game that a girl just out of school should win the two most difficult closed tournaments in the country, the English Nationals and the Surrey Restricted; should take two of the three most difficult European Open titles, the Swedish and the Dutch; and should also tuck away the West Sussex, Wimbledon, Kent, Essex, Surrey and Irish Open crowns. Back home in Holly Lane, Banstead, Mrs Perrin's consumption of silver polish was breaking county records. Who cared? With every blow of the duster, she could content herself with the knowledge that there wasn't a player in the country who could hold a candle to her daughter.

4 Cape Town to Tokyo

'I deem it wise to advise you,' wrote BAE secretary Herbert Scheele to the team, 'that certain inoculations are required for all travellers to South Africa.' Smallpox was essential and yellow fever recommended, he said. For the girls going on to Japan, yellow fever was absolutely essential and cholera was also required. He 'strongly recommended' the team to get their jabs at the BOAC medical centre at Victoria, but Gillian Perrin, leaving nothing to chance, collected her dose at the Hospital for Tropical Diseases, at St Pancras.

With hindsight, an exhausting seven-week tour of South Africa does not seem the ideal way to prepare for the Uber Cup, just one week later. Not even the amount of match practice the tour afforded fully compensated the players, since the standard of badminton in South Africa was not nearly good enough to extend the English team. Gillian emerged from the tour with the odd record of not losing one singles match, but never winning a mixed doubles in the whole Test series.

The team that left Heathrow on the afternoon of April 9th, 1969, was — or should have been — Tony Jordan, Derek Talbot, Ray Sharp, Margaret Boxall, Gillian Perrin and Sue Whetnall. Paul Whetnall, Margaret Beck and Julie Charles were due to join the party in time for the Test series, four weeks later, but in fact there was an unexpected absentee. The new English National singles champion, Ray Sharp, missed the plane. He had a worthy excuse (he was looking after a sick colleague at work), and arrived in Johannesburg twelve hours late, with just a few minutes to spare before going on court for a match against South Transvaal Districts. Not surprisingly, he lost his singles, but pulled through the mixed with Gillian.

Jordan, the team captain, was an astonishing character. Short and stocky (at this time there was even a hint of stoutness about him), he was one of the world's greatest mixed doubles players, winning the All-England in 1968. He very rarely played singles, for which he was not ideally built, but had a remarkable crab-like agility for moving sideways – ideal for doubles, for which in badminton the players more often stand not side by side, but one in front of the other. When they went to South Africa, he already had 92 international caps, which he built to 100 before he retired. He had, Gillian remembers, a great propensity for telling good dirty jokes with a slight speech impediment.

The rest of the team were comparative newcomers to the international scene. For years the British women's game had been dominated by Heather Ward, Ursula Smith and Angela Bairstow, while Roger Mills and Colin Beacom were the outstanding men. With the exception of Jordan, this was the new wave of British champions, but they were to prove far too good for most of their South African opponents.

South Africa is physically a very seductive country. The beauty of the land is staggering (though journeys overland are tempered by Hemingway's MMBA — 'miles and miles of bloody Africa') and the hospitality of the hosts, particularly towards sports visitors from Britain, leaves nothing to be desired but that it should stop once in a while. No sporting encounter seems complete without a large party, no new town can be entered without a reception. For the sake of the sporting peace of mind, it is probably best, once you have agreed to visit the country, to forget the inhuman conditions in which the ruling whites seem for the most part determined to keep the black and coloured masses. Gillian Gilks agrees that at eighteen she probably had no political or social conscience on the matter, though she does have now. The only time they were allowed to play in front of a mixed audience, the Whites were on one side of the court and the non-Whites on the other, and only one non-White coaching clinic was arranged. But staying, as they did, in good hotels or even better homes, the background to the tour was never allowed to intrude on their enjoyment.

On tours like this, the custom is for the visiting nation to pay for the flights in and out, and the host nation to be responsible for accommodation, meals and internal transport. The team's small daily pocket-money allowance did not go far, but as usual the biggest problem on such a tour concerns laundry. When you are travelling all the time, dare you use the laundry service? If you wash your own clothes, will there be time for them to dry before you have to pack them again? The tour had been arranged to coincide with the South African Games, a huge and prolonged festival of sport, held that year in Bloemfontein. For five weeks just about every sport that raises its head in South Africa was given its chance, even to underwater hockey, quoits and angling. Six thousand sportsmen took part, and there would have been many more but for the flood of withdrawals from overseas in protest against the country's apartheid policy. Nevertheless there were some 120 from abroad, including the English badminton team and a handful of leading athletes like Colin Campbell, Howard Payne, John Whetton and Ann Wilson.

The South African badminton championships were held as part of the Games, and there were some surprises. Derek Talbot was the only Briton in the men's semi-finals (he finished third); Jordan and Talbot were beaten in the doubles final by a South African pair; and Jordan and Sue Whetnall lost the mixed final to Talbot and Gillian. She beat Margaret Boxall in the women's singles final, and the Boxall-Whetnall women's team romped through the doubles without losing a set. Gillian was partnered by a South African, Marianne Svensson, and finished third.

After the championships, there were two weeks of travelling round six provinces to play the local teams. Travelling, eating, drinking, sleeping, shopping, sunbathing. Back in Johannesburg for the Eastern Transvaal match, Gillian's diary, painstakingly completed for the folks back home, had an entry for Wednesday April 30th that seemed to typify the whole operation:

> 'Down another mine. Lunch with managers in club. Saw windmill and gardens, slept p.m. in hotel. Cocktail party with mayor. Played E. Transvaal — 7–0. Ray played four times because of Derek's leg (he went to specialist a.m. instead of mine). Others went to Eddie's party. I went back to sleep. Telegram: heard Julie had appendicitis.'

Five days earlier, Derek Talbot had hurt his knee in an exhibition match in Western Province. He was not able to play again until the Second Test, three weeks later, and thereafter was far from his best. Julie Charles (who had just become Julie Rickard) should have come out for the Tests, but in fact had to go straight into the Uber Cup in Tokyo with her fresh appendicitis scar.

The first Test was immediately preceded by a three-day visit to the Kruger National Park, staying in mud huts with oil lamps, rising at 6.00 and going to bed at 9.00. It is, apparently, the best way to see the animals in this 7,000 square mile reserve, where the lions and the elephants reign supreme and nobody gets out of a car. You don't shift your car, either, if there are elephants about. They have been known to charge moving cars, mistaking them for rival elephants!

The five Tests, each one spread over two days, were played within a period of fifteen days in the five major cities of the Union — Johannesburg, Cape Town, Port Elizabeth, East London and Durban. England won them all, though the scores became close at the end: 7–4, 8–3, 7–4, 6–5, 6–5. An analysis of the match results makes it quite clear where England's strength and weakness lay: of the twenty matches in women's singles and doubles, England won nineteen; of the men's twenty, they won only six, and none of those was a singles. The mixed battle went England's way by nine to six, and five of those six defeats were Gillian's pairings with Ray Sharp and Derek Talbot. Sue Whetnall, who played only doubles and mixed, did not lose a match in the whole Test series, and lost only one, a mixed, during the seven weeks of the tour — an astonishing performance.

The three heroines of the tour, with young Margaret Beck, flew off with some confidence on the long journey to Tokyo (where Miss Beck was soon to be known fondly as 'Small Margaret' and Miss Boxall as 'Great Margaret'). The Kent girls, Boxall and Whetnall, decided to lighten their burden by sending some of their luggage direct from South Africa back to London. Unfortunately, by the time they saw it again it had been opened and most of their souvenirs had gone. The flight of the humans was more secure but it was, to be sure, a hell of a journey: from Johannesburg to Perth, via Mauritius; eleven hours later, from Perth to Singapore; thirteen hours later, from Singapore to Tokyo via Bangkok and Hong Kong. They left after breakfast on May 28th and by the time they reached Tokyo it was nearly midnight on May 30th. There they were joined by Heather Nielsen and Julie Rickard, with eight days to go before their first Uber Cup match.

The Uber Cup is, in effect, the women's world team championship and is decided every three years. For it, the badminton-playing world is divided into four geographic zones — America, Europe, Asia and Australasia. The zone winners meet to decide who has the right to enter the Challenge Round. Betty Uber, in her youth a fine lawn tennis player, was one of England's most successful badminton doubles players between the wars — and indeed after the second world war, for she represented the country over a period of 25 years — and she presented the trophy in 1956, after her retirement from the game. Up to six women may play in a team. Each tie is now decided by three singles players, the top two of whom each play twice, and two doubles pairs each playing twice. But in 1969 the tie comprised seven matches, not nine, all played in one evening, so at least one member of the four doubles players had to play three matches within a few hours.

Thailand were the first opponents, the Asian winners, and gave the English girls no trouble. Gillian, Mrs Nielsen and Margaret Boxall played the singles; Boxall-Whetnall and Gillian-Mrs Rickard the doubles. It was a whitewash job, with only one game lost, but the English party knew they would have a different kind of fight on their hands two days later against Indonesia, who had beaten the United States 7–0. The Indonesians had not at that time made their startling mark on world badminton, but the first steps had been firmly taken. Rudy Hartono had won the first of his eight All-England singles titles in 1968 — the same year the intriguingly-named lady Minarni had given Eva Twedberg a fight in the women's final before winning the women's doubles with Retno Kustijah.

To sum up the inter-zone final with cruel haste, Margaret Boxall won her three matches, Gillian Perrin lost her three and — though she didn't know it at the time — Heather Nielsen's single determined the result. She lost. The detailed composition of the tie, of course, was less simple. Mrs Nielsen, playing as third string, had the second match of the tie and by all accounts should never have lost it. Gillian Perrin had to face the mighty Minarni and could hardly have expected to win, though she did expect to win more than two points in the second game. So England ended the singles encounters 2–1 down instead of 2–1 up. The doubles followed, and so did trouble. Sue Whetnall was suffering from tonsillitis, but played nevertheless with Margaret Boxall against the second Indonesian pair. With Miss Whetnall close to collapse at the end of the second game, Miss Boxall just steered her home. Mrs Nielsen took Sue's place for the other doubles, in which the opposition retired at one game all. By that time, Gillian and Julie Rickard had lost both their matches, and indeed at no point did they look like winning them — a dreadful disappointment when they had played so well together in the English season. Gillian was desperately unhappy with her own form — she failed to win a game all night: in those days, she said, she was just not fit enough to survive such a test.

When Japan at last faced Indonesia, it was a one-sided battle marred by some flagrantly dishonest gamesmanship from the challengers. There was no doubt that the finest singles player in the whole tournament was Indonesia's Minarni. She appeared on their draw for the final as the second singles string; their number one was, it seemed, Poppy Tumengkol, whose only appearance in the tournament at that time was as a doubles player against the United States. Poor Miss Tumengkol was obviously going to be sacrificed in order to ensure that Minarni at least won her singles. Japan, with two fairly equal players in Noriko Takagi and Hiroe Yuki (the future and current All-England champions), made no protest. Minarni duly beat Yuki with a superb performance, 11–6, 11–2. What the spectators saw in the next match was a disgrace. Miss Tumengkol won the toss, served once and lost the first game 11–0 in three-and-a-half minutes. At 2–0 in the second, she was hand-in twice, but did not win a point. The match was over in nine minutes and Poppy Tumengkol was in tears at the courtside.

Not many sportsmen get the chance to visit Tokyo, and those who do, don't forget it. It is a most hospitable, highly-expensive, enormous city in which, at most times of the day, it takes hours to get anywhere. The traffic jams are just like home to a Londoner, only more so, but everybody received the extra traffic caused by the Uber Cup tournament with a great big smile. The Governor of Tokyo smiled more broadly than most, and the official translation of his welcoming message in the programme makes clear how much the Japanese enjoy their badminton:

> 'I am great pleased that the 5th World Ladies Badminton Championships for scramble for the Uber Cup will be held under the superintendence of Nippon Badminton Association at Tokyo Gymnasium for 7 days. As you know, Badminton originated from India long ago, was grown at Badminton Village in London, presently, as not only tournament sports but also recreational sports, is extended widely world, and is loved by many people. In Japan, Badminton is spreaded rapidly by efforts of Japanese committee after war, and I have heard that ladies, as world champion, will be challenged by the winner of the inter-zone in this championships. All officials and players participating in this honourable championships from the world, I hope all of you will give full play to your skill and demonstrate sportsmanship in the games and be careful of your health.'

The grammar and the geography may be a little bent, but the message was unmistakable.

5 A bundle of fire

In all her badminton life to this moment, Gillian Perrin had had only one rival of anything like her own age, and that was the Jane Colman of her earliest days in the game. As soon as Gillian drew away from her, no other youngster approached her in talent or achievement. As an absurdly young senior, she had been engaged, as we have seen, in trying to pop off the champions of the previous generation. Of those, only Heather Nielsen remained at the top. The only other British players Gillian was ever likely to lose to were her contemporaries in the England squad, Margaret Boxall (who in the summer of 1969 was 24) and Sue Whetnall (26). At 19, Gillian was almost certain to outlast them — and was indeed already recognised as a better all-round player than either — and the domestic pressure on her could only come from below. And so we come to a small name, and a small person, who was to plague Gillian's attempts at supremacy for many years to come: Beck.

Margaret Beck was a Cumberland girl, 18 months younger than Gillian and still, naturally, the All-England Junior champion. Probably the smallest world-class player outside Japan, she was then just over 5ft 1in tall, but weighed 8 stone 4 lb — at the time, two pounds more than Gillian, who was seven inches taller. While Gillian was a junior, Miss Beck was never a significant threat to her, though her determination and energy were boundless and she once took nine points off her in a final. She was extraordinarily mobile, very much faster about the court than Gillian and with a power of shot that was surprising for her size. She had an aggressive match temperament which often led to frustration when she was playing against 'runners' — the indefatigable retrievers who go on and on getting the shuttle back. Gillian's superior stroke play gave her a greater chance of beating such opponents as Eva Twedberg, the Swedish All-England champion of 1968 and 1971, than Maggie Beck could ever conjure up by her industry. She was, as Gillian herself put it, a little bundle of fire, and very good to watch.

At 18, she had already played in the Uber Cup team in Japan, and was to cause a sensation in the Edinburgh Commonwealth Games that followed the 1969–70 badminton season. As that season progressed, she was not landing any major trophies, but she was securing a few notable scalps in the open tournaments. As one of Gillian's two official doubles partners (Julie Rickard was the other), she was also reaching a good many finals — though they did not actually win a tournament together the whole season.

Of the leading open singles titles, Gillian (who was now working in the public relations department of the Automobile Association head office) won the English Nationals, the Wimbledon, the Kent and the Northern. The Nationals were held in Poole, Dorset, and attracted only nine female singles competitors. Six of them were internationals, and all nine came from the south of England. At that time the competitive element in women was not what it is now. The players of the Midlands and North, knowing quite surely where the winner was coming from, did not think it worth while to offer even token opposition. Among the nine, incidentally, was a lady named Sue Gilks, whose husband Gillian was later to marry. Of the other tournaments, Heather Nielsen won the Surrey Open, Margaret Boxall the London and the Scottish, and Sue Whetnall the Dutch during which a smoke bomb was let off in protest against South Africa's participation in the championships. Ten years later, Gillian remembered her Dutch semi with Sue as the closest match she ever played: 12–11, 11–12, 12–11. And so to the three biggest tournaments of the season: the All-England, the European and the Commonwealth Games.

For four years, you may remember, Gillian had never won a singles at the All-England. At last she made it. Seeded again, she put out Eva Carlsen and Joke van Beusekom before losing 12–11 in the third to Jette Foge, of Denmark. Gillian was leading the decider at 9–5 when, according to *The Times*, she was clearly overcome by an attack of nerves. Meanwhile in the other half of the draw, Maggie Beck (unseeded) was putting the mighty to the sword. She beat the seeded Imre Nielsen in the first round, the experienced Japanese Hiroe Amano in the second, and the highly-seeded United States champion, Tyna Barinaga, in the quarter-final. By the time Heather Nielsen sent her packing in the semi-final, Maggie had made a mark on world badminton that was never to be erased. She was, incidentally, just 13 years younger than Mrs Nielsen, who only delayed Etsuko Takenaka for 15 minutes in the final — one of the rare unseeded All-England singles champions.

Gillian and Roger Mills lost their mixed title, being narrowly beaten in the semi by the eventual winners, Per Walsoe and Pernille Malgaard Hansen, and with Julie Rickard she lost a close doubles final to the everlasting enemy, Boxall and Whetnall. For the European championships four weeks later, in Port Talbot, the pairings were changed: Talbot was Gillian's partner for the mixed, and Maggie Beck for the doubles. Miss Beck and Miss Boxall were the singles nominations, and Miss Boxall put out the European champion, Irmgard Latz. However, neither survived the semi-finals, and England's gold medals were brought home by the long-established partnership of Margaret Boxall and Sue Whetnall, and the new one of David Eddy and Mrs Whetnall. Eddy was brought in to replace the old warrior, Tony Jordan, who had just won his 100th cap after 18 years of playing for England.

As the season ended, the BAE issued their first official ranking list, which thereafter came out annually. The name of Gillian Perrin was firmly at the top, followed by Miss Boxall and Mrs Nielsen (jointly second), Miss Beck, Mrs Whetnall, Mrs Palmer (formerly Angela Bairstow, still hanging on) and Mrs Rickard. All except Mrs Nielsen, who left to live abroad, and Mrs Palmer were selected for the Commonwealth Games team, and Gillian and Margaret Boxall were subsequently named as top seeds for the singles. The five men were Eddy, Mills, Sharp, Talbot and Whetnall, and all ten in due course received a notice of three practice meetings to be held before the Games in July. It was couched in terms even less courteous than those of team manager Jack McColl's previous missive:

> 'These practices are for *your* benefit. Will Messrs Eddy, Sharp and Talbot please have the good manners to be early, so that other members of the team who care do not have their time wasted, and the BAE does not waste the money provided by small clubs throughout the country. At the time of writing, 15th June, Monday, a.m., I still do not have photos or medical forms returned from Rickard and Sharp. If these do not arrive in my hands by 17th Wednesday, the two people concerned will *not* be entered in the Games.'

All was well in the end, and of course England emerged with medals galore: silver and bronze in the men's singles, which was unexpectedly won by the Canadian, Jamie Paulson (whom nine years later Gillian identified on the BBC programme 'A Question of Sport' by his celebrated line, 'My father's a millionaire, but today I'm the richer man by far'); all three medals in the women's singles and the mixed; and the first two in the women's doubles. Apart from Paulson's fine win, the men's singles was notable for the fact that the two top seeds, Malaysians Punch Gunalan and Abdul Tahman, were both beaten by Englishmen, Whetnall and Sharp — surprisingly, the first occasion in the history of the game in which an English player had beaten a ranked Malaysian in competition.

In Edinburgh, Gillian's partnership with Roger Mills was restored, but they lost the final to Talbot and Boxall, 8–15, 15–12, 15–12. Nor was her female partner the same as she had been in the European: this time she and Julie Rickard reached the final, to lose once more to Boxall and Whetnall. And the women's singles final? Beck versus Perrin, of course, and there would not have been much money on Beck. But the little one made it, for an astonishing victory. It was the first time she had ever beaten Gillian, and it was doubly galling for the older girl that her defeat should come at such a moment.

She still looks back on it as one of her very worst days: 'It was awful, a massive disappointment. I should have won that gold.' She started well enough, against an acutely nervous Beck, who served out of court three times in the first game and lost it 3–11. Then in the second she put on a performance of the highest class, and won 11–3. Perrin went 5–1 up in the third, but it was Beck who reached match point at 10–7. Five times she was within a stroke of the gold medal, and five times she was frustrated. But she made it, 11–8. The fighter was triumphant, the artist subdued. How hard it must be to congratulate your opponent when you have just suffered the greatest disappointment of your life.

Suitable refreshment for the winner, at 18, of the Dutch Open. But in the summer of 1970 (below), *one of the great disappointments of her life: beaten by Margaret Beck* (centre) *in the Commonwealth Games singles final. Bronze medallist was Margaret Boxall* (right)

Gillian Gilks and Margaret Beck at Wembley after winning the 1974 All-England doubles title

From this moment on, for years and years and years, nothing else in badminton seemed of much consequence beside the Beck-Perrin rivalry — though accurately, it swiftly became the Beck-Gilks rivalry. Two months after the Commonwealth Games, still only 20, Gillian married Michael Gilks, whose first marriage had been dissolved. This brought her a problem she may not have expected, and brought it soon: the wedding was variously reported as bringing her the name of Gilks, Gilkes, Jilks and even Gelks, and you would be surprised how long that lasted. *The Times* gave her a Jilks in March 1971, and the *Telegraph* in November 1972. Even the *Birmingham Evening News*, in whose area she went to live, long remained undecided. It was not only on paper that the doubt was expressed. The 'G' in Gillian was soft, as in Jill, we all knew that; but what about Gilks? Was it indeed Jilks, or hard as in gilt?

Michael Gilks (soft, as in Gillian) was 29, an engineer in the electrical supply industry. A badminton enthusiast who, like so many, could not give enough time to practice to enable him to reach his full potential, he became nationally known as an umpire. They had met during the Worcestershire Open at Barnt Green (where they later lived for two years) in October, 1969, married the next September and parted in the spring of 1976. Badminton brought them together and badminton forced them apart. Michael practised with Gillian, often travelled with her and, as she readily acknowledged, supported her all the way with the game. In the end, it was too much. There were too many pressures, too many tensions. It is not easy to marry anyone whose life is controlled by a sport.

'Afterwards he blamed badminton,' Gillian said, 'and you can understand that. He said we would have had kids but for badminton. There were misunderstandings, a lack of communication. I'm not very good at communicating, at sitting down and talking it out, unless there's someone to draw it out of me. I go back into my shell.'

Gillian had sometime earlier given up her job at the AA and turned to temporary secretarial work through an agency, which gave her the time she needed for practice and training. After her marriage she became, as the local papers had it, 'Birmingham housewife Gillian Gilks' (or possibly Gelkes), earning a few pounds with a bit of typing and a bit of coaching at schools, and for a while at Birmingham University. But this season, like so many others to follow, she was going to have her hands full trying to re-establish herself as England's leading player. Too much work would get in the way.

The season did not start too well. By the end of November, 1970, Maggie Beck had won the Worcestershire, Wimbledon, Northern and Warwickshire Opens. Gillian had met her in only one of them, but twice had lost in semi-finals to Tyna Barinaga. Gillian had been preferred for the match against West Germany, but had lost the singles. Beck was picked for the next international, against Scotland. The doubles had been going as well as ever, the women's with Beck and the mixed with either Mills or Talbot; but two other significant female partners were about to arise. Judy Hashman had arisen long since, and had played with Gillian before, but the partnership took on greater importance with the news that Mrs Hashman, an American, had become a British citizen. Even at the age of 35, it was going to be difficult to keep her out of the national squad. The other name was a new one, the new All-England Junior champion, Nora Gardner. At 16, her all-round talents were making the sort of impact that Gillian's had four years earlier. In the Wimbledon Open in November, she substituted at the last moment as Tyna Barinaga's doubles partner, and they won the tournament. She played with Gillian for the first time in the English Nationals in December, and they lost the final to Beck and Rickard.

One should not lose sight of the fact that, while the most glamorous route to the top of the game is through winning the open tournaments, as strong and secure a footing is to be found on the parallel path of county badminton. Gillian's county of Surrey, for which she continued to play wherever she lived, had for many years been overwhelmingly the strongest in the land, able often to leave internationals out of its team. During the 1960s, Kent and Essex provided the stiffest opposition, and in November 1970, Kent were able to field a side that beat Surrey by ten matches to seven. And what a side, to include Paul Whetnall, Ray Sharp, Margaret Boxall and Sue Whetnall. For what seems to be the only time in her career, Gillian (who almost automatically won all her county games) was shattered to lose them all — the singles to Boxall, and both doubles to the combinations of Boxall and the Whetnalls. How could it possibly be that, when the two counties next met only two months later, the score was 15–0 to Surrey, and at the end of the season Kent were relegated to the second division?

It was because the four Kent stars who between them won ten matches in a county tie dived into a disastrously premature attempt to set up a professional badminton circus in Britain. Organised by John Beirne, of Southampton, the two Whetnalls, Margaret Boxall, Ray Sharp and the American, Tyna Barinaga, announced in October that, as from December 1st, they would be leaving the amateur game to play and coach as professionals. The players were on four-year contracts, but within two years they had applied for reinstatement as amateurs. At the time he launched the circus, Beirne said: 'I hope to do for badminton what Jack Kramer did for lawn tennis.' Well, he tried. They all tried, but almost everything was against them.

They were five fine players, certainly five of the best ten players then in Britain, but apart from Miss Barinaga they were very familiar figures to all badminton enthusiasts. We had been watching them play each other in open tournament finals for years – why should we suddenly fork out good money for the privilege? Had there been another five players from Europe and the East, it might have been a different story, but there is a limit to the number of times you can watch Paul Whetnall and Ray Sharp beating each other. The idea was that these people should show the way and others would follow, but the others were not ready to follow then, as they might have done ten years later. As to the coaching, that had its appeal; but good coaching was available more cheaply elsewhere. And for financial security, the group seemed to be backed with promises more surely than with any more marketable commodity.

So the move failed, but you can imagine the effect it had on England's national squad for the two years they were out. No wonder the BAE were delighted to see Judy Hashman changing her coat! One year later the woman who had played for the United States for 12 years found herself captain of the British Uber Cup team. (The letter of invitation to the squad in December 1970, by the way, came from BAE secretary Brian Bisseker and was couched in far more acceptable terms than the last one: 'It must be recognised that for a scheme of this sort to have any value at all, either to the BAE or to the players, self-imposed self-discipline by all the players is a pre-requisite and is essential, and this must be accepted by the players ...')

Meanwhile, more than half Gillian's doubles tournaments were played with Mrs Hashman, a third with Maggie Beck and the rest divided between Julie Rickard, Jenny Horton and Nora Gardner. The sudden removal of the Kent contingent seemed to inspire Gillian to her best badminton, and at the beginning of December she beat Miss Beck three times in one week: in the finals of the English Nationals, the London Open and in the county match against Middlesex, for whom Beck had been playing since she came down from Cumberland. That made up for a few past sorrows, but the new ranking list issued by the BAE still had Maggie Beck at its head, followed by Gillian, Julie Rickard, Jenny Horton and Barbara Giles, a new young name who was to play a central role in Gillian's battles with the establishment some years later. *The Daily Telegraph* found the ranking 'an extraordinary mixture of past, present and future'. According to their correspondent, Jenny Horton (who used to be Jenny Pritchard) had not played one significant singles match in the past four years. The whole thing, they said, 'abounds with inconsistencies'.

There it was, anyway, and from January to March the brilliant rivals battered away at each other and at anyone else who got in the way. They seldom played a really good match against each other, but still managed to combine well enough in doubles. But then, history shows that almost anybody is liable to win the doubles with Gilks as a partner. In the three months to the end of the season, Gillian was in seven doubles finals with three partners and won five of them; she was in seven mixed finals with two partners and won five of them.

As usual, the 1971 All-England was the climax of the season, and a disappointing one it was for the English. Both Gillian and Miss Beck lost in the fourth round of the singles, where Gillian's opponent was the joint top seed, Noriko Takagi of Japan. Despite making a good, crisp start, she went out 11–8, 11–1. Takagi was a 'runner'. Once she got the hang of Gillian's superior stroke play, she began getting to the shuttles and returning them and returning them and returning them. As can so easily happen when the player cannot be advised by a courtside expert, Gillian couldn't see what was happening. Strokes that used to be winners were winners no longer, so she tried harder and harder to make them winners, playing them tighter and tighter and therefore making more and more mistakes. Not until it was all over did someone point out what had been happening, and what should have happened: that Gillian should have relaxed and been prepared to play out the rallies, waiting to execute the right stroke at the right time. It's always easy afterwards.

Gillian reached both the doubles finals and lost them both. Judy Hashman had to play the women's with torn ligaments in her racket arm, for which she was given a pain-killing injection half-an-hour before the game. With that appalling handicap, they lost by only 15–10, 18–13 to Takagi and Hiroe Yuki. Gillian and Derek Talbot led the holders, Svend Pri and Ulla Strand, by 9–6 in the third game, but went down 15–12, 8–15, 15–11. And that was more or less that for the season, except that Surrey won the county championship again — the 15th time in 17 years!

The season that was coming up, 1971–72, was to be a long and hard one. It included the Uber Cup before the All-England and the European championships after it, and even then it wasn't time to rest: badminton had been chosen as one of the demonstration games in the Munich Olympics, and there was no doubt that England would be providing some of the competitors for that tournament. During the summer of '71, the BAE appointed Roger Mills chief coach and they also organised a new event, sponsored by Granwood Flooring: a two-day round-robin at Guildford, with which the season opened.

It's worth looking at this in detail, for it was the first of its kind (the sponsorship was later continued by the Hearts of Oak Building Society). It was a singles tournament only, for which the BAE invited 32 men and 16 women. In groups of four (one player was seeded to each group, and in only two of the twelve cases failed to prove the winner) they were to play each other for eleven hours on Saturday, 9th October. Group winners then went into a knock-out competition on Sunday. It was clearly a prestige event, and one which the leading players could hardly afford to miss, but it was clear they were likely to emerge, once again, with a hole in the pocket.

The two winners would each be given a prize voucher to the value of — wait for it — £5, together with a memento and the loan of the perpetual trophy for a year. The runners-up would have a £2.50 prize. There would be no subsistence allowance, despite the fact that play would not end till 11.00 p.m. on Saturday night, and a contribution towards travel expenses would only be made to those players travelling a long distance; but a limited amount of private hospitality was being arranged. There was nothing particularly unusual in these arrangements — indeed it was a bonus to the players that they were not required to submit an entry fee on this occasion – but it does give one an idea of what it cost to play badminton at the top in the early 1970s.

The gap between the two leading women players and the rest (though the absentees did include Mrs Hashman) was never so apparent. In their three pool matches, each involving the best of three games, Beck and Gilks each lost an absolute total of twelve points. They went on, of course, to meet in the final, where Maggie Beck played at her best to dominate the match. Two weeks later, Christina Wood noted in *The Guardian* that the battle between these two for the top singles berth in the Uber Cup had begun: Gillian defeated Maggie equally heavily in the Worcestershire final, and the next month in the Northern. Beck struck back by winning the Warwickshire, the Wimbledon Open (in which Gillian was put out early by a Dutch girl) and, in December 1971, by taking from Gillian the English National singles title that she had held for three years. Gillian never had any problem in responding on the doubles court (she won the women's national doubles title for the first time and the mixed for the fourth time in five years), but so far it was definitely one up to Miss Beck.

Maggie did not contest the London Open, leaving Gillian free to retain her hat-trick of titles, but Beck was named for the only singles place in the internationals against Denmark in Copenhagen, where she beat Lene Koppen, and against Sweden in Stockholm, where she lost to Eva Twedberg. Every week now brought a new battle: Beck lost the final of the Swedish Open to Twedberg, and Gillian won both doubles titles; Beck beat Gilks in the Scottish final, and Gillian won both doubles. Within days, the two had met in a county match again, and Gillian swept her rival aside with contemptuous ease. 'We seldom had a decent match,' Gillian recalled. 'It was nearly always one-sided, one way or the other.'

At this moment the English selectors made an astonishing decision. Judy Hashman, who as *The Times* correspondent had recently put it, had virtually retired from singles play, was at 36 years of age going to play both doubles and singles for England in the Uber Cup, as well as leading the team. The outcome of the tie, a European semi-final against Holland, was never in doubt, but the only match England lost was the Hashman singles, 11–4, 11–5 to Agnes van der Muelen-Geene. For the final against Denmark, Julie Rickard came in to play the third singles. That didn't affect the outcome either: Gillian won her singles against Anne Berglund, and her doubles with Mrs Hashman, but nobody else on the side won a game, never mind a match.

Coming only ten days before the All-England, that didn't do a lot for the confidence of the natives, though some compensation was at hand. In the often-infuriating fixture arranged at the beginning of the All-England week itself, England met Japan at Carlisle, the first time the two nations had met in a bi-sexual international match. Since the Japanese had only two male players in England, the encounter was weighted heavily on the distaff side and, to general surprise, England won 5–2. Hiroe Yuki beat Maggie Beck in a close fight, but Gillian had no trouble with Machiko Aizawa. For reasons that must have made some sense to somebody, Gillian was in Carlisle partnered by Julie Rickard in the doubles, though three days later she was going to be playing with Judy Hashman; Maggie Beck, who was to be Mrs Rickard's partner in the All-England, was against Japan paired with Mrs Hashman.

Both English pairs won in the friendly, Gilks and Rickard with difficulty against Yuki and Mrs Nakayama (the All-England champions), Beck and Hashman with even greater difficulty against Aizawa and Takenaka. At Wembley, alas, the Aizawa-Takenaka combination proved too strong for Mrs Hashman when partnered by Gillian instead of Maggie (in the semi-final) and too strong in the final for Maggie when partnered by Julie Rickard. What a confusing and disappointing mess! England contested all three doubles finals at Wembley, through Stevens and Tredgett, Gillian and Talbot, and Beck and Rickard, but lost them all.

The singles were no more satisfying to the Britons. Gillian faced the former holder, Hiroe Yuki, in the second round and in the third game, when she was leading 3–0, sank into one of her inexplicable moods in which she loses concentration and drive. Miss Beck survived to the fourth, where she was comprehensively beaten by the eventual winner, Mrs Nakayama (formerly Miss Takagi).

Apart from Surrey squeezing home 9–8 in the county final against Essex, that was the end of the 1971–72 domestic season. Off, straight away, to the European Championships in Sweden. For the first time, these opened with team championships, the individual results in which have nothing to do with subsequent individual progress in the competition — fortunately, since during England's crucial 3–2 win over Sweden, which led to their winning the title, Gillian lost to Eva Twedberg. In the semi-final of the individual tournament, Gillian beat her 11–2, 11–7, which rated as the upset of the week. Maggie Beck was waiting for her in the final, and secured her most overwhelming win: 11–0, 11–1. Gillian came home with two gold medals: with Mrs Hashman she beat Beck and Rickard in the doubles, and with Talbot she won the mixed — not losing a game in the course of either contest. Overall, it was an excellent week for England, and it concluded what had been an impressive season.

Gillian had established beyond doubt that she was the finest doubles player in the country, and indeed in Europe. Margaret Beck, still only 20 years old, had undeniably outplayed her on the singles court. Within five months the skirmishing would start all over again, at the opening of a new and quite extraordinary season — a visit to Moscow, the first visit by the Chinese, a tour of Japan and then an All-England tournament the like of which had not been seen for 35 years. But in this off-season, there was a unique event: badminton was played at the Olympic Games in Munich as a demonstration event — a gesture made to games that wanted, and seemed suited, to become official Olympic sports. Entry to the Munich tournament was designed to give all the leading badminton nations a showing. Britain was represented by Gillian Gilks, Elliot Stuart and Derek Talbot, and Gilks and Talbot won the mixed doubles. It brought them gold medals and much confusing coverage in their local papers, which seemed convinced that the medals were as good as anyone else's. It also brought them the horrible experience of the Israeli massacre and the lasting memory that they had walked past the block in which the athletes were being held hostage, late in that fateful night.

6 Hot air and other hazards

There isn't an indoor game in the book that can be so affected as badminton by the conditions in which it is played. 'The great joy about badminton,' people tell you, 'is that you can play it anywhere.' That is also one of its great problems. Because it is so easy to mark the court and put up a net, because at a social level the equipment is comparatively inexpensive, and because the game is, simply, such fun to play even for the inexpert, people do tend to play almost anywhere. Those of us without pretensions to skill welcome that fact. On a calm day, a firm, sandy beach makes a delightful court, though to spot a high shuttle coming out of the sun is a bit testing. Your back garden does not have to be anything like as carefully nursed for badminton as it does for tennis; almost anything goes, barring rabbit-holes, and if there is a bit of a breeze it sharpens your reactions no end.

After that sort of preparation, to play in the village hall is some kind of paradise, but oddly enough it is here that your problems begin. You feel obliged to take the game rather more seriously, and you begin to be annoyed at the unyielding restrictions that hem you in. Your steepling retrieval shots are no good now: the ceiling is no more than 15 feet up and festooned with large, hanging metal lampshades. Even if you gather up all the chairs and stack them on the stage, you are still going to crack the wall — or possibly a window — with your backswing when you are forced to the baseline. Adjust your game, learn tolerance, and reflect that it could be much worse. Ian Maconachie, one of the very best players ever to come from Ireland, tells marvellous stories about badminton in England 60 years ago, when experienced players used to do their best to spread the gospel by playing exhibitions in deprived and innocent areas.

Village hall lighting then was a real laugh. They once found four-foot lengths of gas piping suspended low over the net on each side of the court, each one with eight naked gas mantles. The illuminations had been specially installed for the occasion, and had used up the entire stock of mantles from the village store. Pretty soon an erratic backhand drive swept along one of the pipes, taking with it eight brand new mantles.

Much more sophisticated arrangements had been made at the next village on the tour. Electricity had arrived! An odd collection of bulbs hung around the walls, the light from which just about reached the centre of the court. The standard of light was not exactly steady: outside a car, its rear wheels jacked up in the air, was roaring away, driving a dynamo. Ultimately, of course, it fell off the jacks and that was the end of all lighting, but that was not the most memorable aspect of play in that hall. In the exact centre of the court was an army stove, its chimney pipe going straight up through the roof. The net was in two halves, tied to the pipe. At such times the genius of improvisation decends on the player. (It couldn't have been a great deal better, by all accounts, when the game was first played in the hall of Badminton House more than a century ago, and the net stretched from the fireplace to the front door with the butler having to ring before he came in.)

When your primitive badminton days are behind you, it is still by no means uncommon to play in halls where, even if the roof itself reaches 25 or 30 ft the supporting beams and girders are very much lower. The proliferation of purpose-built sports centres in the past 10 years means that first-class tournaments are now nearly always played without ceiling problems, but even as late as 1968, when Judy Hashman wrote her book 'Badminton: a Champion's Way', she included a page of serious and detailed advice on the best method of delivering high serves through a network of girders. Basically, she had decided that it was safer to maintain the natural rhythm and direction of the serve and apologise in advance for the let, if it came, than to make an effort to alter the strength or angle of the stroke in order to get the shuttle through a particular gap.

Extremes of temperature are frequently met, in centrally-heated Europe as much as in Indonesia. (Mrs Hashman once practised in the United States on a court where it was 13 degrees below freezing; she wore trousers, three sweaters, hat, scarf and gloves.) Damp courts are as great a menace in badminton as in squash, and to the class player at least, the intensity and positioning of the lights (even when they are out of range of the shuttle) is a critical factor, because of the frequency with which players are likely to have to focus on the descent of a high shuttle. At that level of play, however, you hear no sharper criticism than that directed to 'drift'.

This can be caused by something as simple as high wind outside the building and an open door somewhere, but in large, highly-populated halls the cause is often more complex and its effect more disturbing. Reducing it to basics, it is usually down to the hot air above the crowd rising to the highest point it can find before it cools, and the air it displaces swirling down to take its place. In arenas that lie within buildings as vast as Wembley there is additional movement caused by the air from the surrounding areas rushing in to join the fun, and in the early part of the week of the All-England championships, when seven courts are in use, the two at each end of the arena suffer quite ludicrously from the Wembley drift. Badminton players used to think that the movement of the shuttle there, which could often be as much as 18 inches from a high shot, was the ultimate in the horrors they had to face. That, however, was before they began playing in the Albert Hall.

The drift there, said Gillian Gilks, who played in the first Friends' Provident

Masters in 1979, was 'absolutely diabolical. You really wouldn't believe it if you hadn't tried to play there yourself.' It frequently made something of a fiasco of the second games, as it affected one end of the court much more than the other. Also, aggravatingly, it changed its nature completely between the day of practice and the first day of competition.

If you can cure, or overcome, all those hazards, you are left with the background, which when you are looking for a shuttle can be very important indeed. On a bright day, windows in the walls or roof of the hall can be fiendishly awkward, particularly if they cause the shuttle to pass across a glaring patch between two darker ones. Brightly painted walls are just as bad: unlike the batsman, the badminton player likes to see a plain, dark colour ahead of him against which the white shuttle stands out well. Which brings us to spectators, of which, like a batsman, the badminton player would rather not be aware. In a small hall, there aren't likely to be any, because there won't be any room for them. In a big arena, with a perfectly sprung floor and excellent lighting, they may be all around you.

'Hopefully,' said Gillian, 'the lighting is so arranged that they remain in darkness, at least compared to the amount of light on the court. If they are not, and there is much movement during the game, it can be very distracting. But you'd be surprised how much gets cut out, when you are concentrating properly. Often you don't even hear them. By the time a long rally is over and they are cheering, you are breathing in more oxygen and it's pounding in your ears and you can't hear a thing. By the time you've calmed down, so have they. Personally, I don't get particularly lifted by crowd support and I don't mind if there's nobody there at all. The thing that can really destroy your concentration is just one person walking round the courtside, so close that you just can't shut them out.

'In the Dutch Open of 1972, the Dutch girl, Joke van Beusekom, got mad at a TV cameraman at the edge of the court. She had to get the referee to move him, and by then she was so wild she was really hammering the shuttle. She smashed everything right through me — it was the only time I ever lost to her.'

There were no errant TV cameramen in the Dutch Open of 1973, when Gillian met Joke in the final and beat her 11–2, 12–11. (Gillian won all the other Dutch titles too. But by then, there had been all kinds of excitement in the season. It opened with the Granwood round-robin tournament again, which closed with the same two winners as in the first year, Maggie Beck and Ray Stevens. It was notable once more for the absolute ease with which the three leading women, Beck, Gilks and Nielsen, brushed aside the other 13 players; and for the major upset in the semi-final in which the former junior champion, Keith Arthur, beat the England number one, Derek Talbot. The men then whitewashed Holland in a Thomas Cup match before the top two players of each sex whipped off for a quick weekend in Moscow. They very easily won the two friendlies they played against the Soviet Union, but were impressed at the strength of the Soviet men's play. It was the first time a British team had been invited there, and their reactions after three days were much the same as many other British reactions proved to be after a much longer stay in 1980: surprise at the warm friendliness of the people, the queues in the shops, the matrons on the hotel floors, the magnificence of Red Square and the fact that taking pictures of Russian policemen is definitely not on. The queues in the stores are even more surprising. You are supposed to queue to select the goods, elsewhere to pay for them, and again to collect them. Ignorant of the system, Gillian innocently jumped all three queues when she went shopping for fur hats.

Back home, the usual exchange of singles titles went on between Beck and Gilks, with Gillian winning the Warwickshire and the Lancashire, and Maggie the Wimbledon and the National. The last was one of their closer matches — 11–5, 5–11, 11–6. Gillian's doubles performance was again quite staggering: with Derek Talbot withdrawing from their partnership because of 'flu, she played the mixed with David Hunt, a man with whom she had never played before. They won without conceding a game. The stupendous partnership of Mike Tredgett and Nora Gardner had not then been formed. Tredgett was playing with Miss Gardner's Essex team mate Barbara Giles, and Nora was then engaged in a not particularly successful partnership with Phil Smith. Gardner and Giles together had become an excellent team, and they had a thunderous semi-final with Gillian and Judy Hashman, the holders: 13–15, 15–0, 15–13. Winning the doubles final much more easily, against Beck and Rickard, gave Gillian her tenth National title in six years, at the age of 22. It was already clear that Nora Gardner was an outstanding player, but twice in two months Gillian beat her in county matches: 11–0, 11–0 and 11–1, 11–5. One other result on the sidelines deserves a note: the All-England Under-15 singles and doubles titles were won by a 12-year-old from Surrey, Karen Bridge.

The new year opened with intense activity for Gillian Gilks. From the Swedish Open (both doubles titles) she hurried back to England for the historic Chinese tour. No British player had seen the Chinese play badminton, but there was not one who was not left apprehensive, if not positively pessimistic, at his chances of success by the tales of Chinese skill relayed from the Far East. These were confirmed by the statistics from Denmark, which the party had visited on their way to London: they beat Denmark in every one of their four encounters, by match scores of 10–0, 8–2, 8–2. It was a party of ten inscrutable Chinese who arrived at Heathrow, to be welcomed by, among others, Tommy Marrs. The impression of a rather dull, serious-minded, humourless bunch was inescapable, he recalls, with their identical, sexless, high-buttoned 'Chairman Mao' suits and their absolutely endless politeness. But soon everyone succumbed to their charm. 'Friendship first, victory second' was always their slogan, and of course they achieved both without difficulty.

Most were teachers or physical culture students, and none was younger than 23. The two men who played their singles in the first match, at Crystal Palace, were both 30 years old, but their play was some way from being geriatric. England won only two of the seven matches — the two Gilks doubles encounters — and nobody else won even a game against the visitors, who often had to be generous to concede a point. The English players were stunned and the Press lost in admiration. Dicky Rutnagur wrote in *The Daily Telegraph*: 'There can be no talk of England's weaknesses. The overall margin and the measure of the visitors' superiority was due entirely to their exceptional ability. They wield their rackets deftly, but at the crux of their skill is remarkable speed. The Chinese veer quickly to the opponent's stroke and reach the shuttlecock so soon they have added time for choice of shot.'

On their way to their next engagement, at Bristol, the Chinese dropped in on the Duchess of Beaufort at Badminton House (the Duke was out hunting) to see where it all began. They also had an appointment with Harlech Television in Bristol, whose executives were delighted to see the Chinese party step out of a black limousine at the door of the studios. They were escorted with due honour to the programme suite, where it was discovered they were members of the staff of a Chinese restaurant in Warminster, hoping to buy tickets for the international. There were eight matches in Bristol (where the event opened officially the Whitchurch Sports Centre) and England won three of them — Gillian's two doubles and a second women's doubles. Once again, all the other matches were two-game wins for the Chinese. And talking, as we were, about temperature: it was between 45 and 50 degrees Fahrenheit in the unheated main hall — just about right for the players, but overcoat weather for the spectators.

By the time they went to Carlisle, the visitors were beginning to get the measure of our doubles play. Gillian and Maggie Beck won in straight games, but for the first time Gillian and Derek Talbot lost, as did all the other doubles pairs: 7–1. Same again in the last of the tour matches, at Birmingham, though this time both Miss Beck, in the singles, and the second women's doubles pair of Hashman and Nielsen managed to win a game. Friendship was never absent in the overwhelming victories, but as Talbot said, it's not too difficult to smile when you're kicking hell out of your opponent. It was Talbot, incidentally, who pointed out to a journalist that so entirely amateur was England's badminton that he was required to take 10 days off work in order to play in the four tour matches.

With hardly time to go home and pack a bigger case, Gillian was off to Japan. Almost every year, a women's team from the West is invited there, and in January 1973 it was a mixed European bunch: Gillian, Eva Twedberg from Sweden, Joke van Beusekom from Holland, Marieluise Zizmann from Germany and the Flindt sisters from Denmark. The result of the five-rubber series depended on the last meeting, in Tokyo, and the headline in the *Herald-Tribune* said it all: 'Japan Nips Europe Team in Final Badminton Meet'. Gillian did not have the happiest of times with her health, but emerged reasonably well with one singles won and one lost, and three doubles won and one lost.

Between that tour and the All-England, Gillian had a triple win in the Dutch Open and a win over Maggie Beck in the final of the Surrey Open. That made it 3–3 in their meetings that season and gave Gillian an extraordinary record: in 10 tournaments, two of which were overseas opens, she had won all three titles six times and both doubles on the other four occasions. Never can England have had such a successful No. 2 player.

The pre-All-England match this year was something a bit different: Europe v Asia in Edinburgh, bringing some encounters that could have considerable relevance to Wembley. Quite astonishingly, the Europeans won 8–2, losing only the two men's doubles matches. Among the singles wins were those of Eva Twedberg (Sweden) and Svend Pri (Denmark) against the two top seeds for Wembley, Hiroe Yuki and Rudy Hartono; among the doubles successes was the emphatic win by Beck and Gilks over the All-England title holders, Aizawa and Takenaka. British representation at Wembley was boosted by the fact that the four Kent players who two years earlier had left the amateur fold, had been accepted back by the BAE. They included the former holders of the women's doubles title, Margaret Boxall and Sue Whetnall, who had the misfortune to be drawn against each other in the singles first round.

The tournament opened with a severe dose of bad luck for two English players. Ray Stevens never reached the starting line, laid low by tonsillitis (he and Tredgett had been doubles finalists in 1972), and the newly-returned Paul Whetnall had to retire with a badly-pulled tendon when on the brink of glory. Whetnall had won his first match easily enough and seemed about to put out the fifth seed, Muljadi of Indonesia, when he dropped without warning and gave up, leading 11–4 in the third. Gillian Gilks dismissed the young Japanese student, Miss Nishio, with embarrassing ease, 11–0, 11–0. Being regarded as second-class citizens in their own country (a situation to which they do not seem to object), the less experienced Japanese and Malaysian girls often lack confidence on foreign courts to a drastic degree. Once they begin to slide, it is not unusual to see them totally disintegrate. Gillian reached the semi-final after beating two Danes and a German for the loss of only one game, but in the other half of the draw Maggie Beck was even more devastating. She lost only three points in the first round and four in the second before beating Sue Whetnall 11–3, 11–8 and former holder Etsuko Takenaka 11–3, 11–3.

At the same stage in the men's singles only one European, Svend Pri, was left. The women's line-up was positively encouraging for Western badminton: Gilks v Yuki, Beck v Koppen. Beck and Gilks were one of three European couples in the women's doubles semis, and the mixed held three British pairs and one Danish. By the Friday night nothing could possibly have been better for Gillian: she had reached all three finals, and in the singles would play Maggie Beck in the first all-English All-England singles final for 35 years. Miss Beck took only 16 minutes to beat Lene Koppen, and Mrs Gilks, in one of her most concentrated and composed performances at Wembley, swept the top seed aside 11–4, 11–5.

According to *The Daily Telegraph* on Monday, 'Gillian Gilks, poor girl, was too overawed by her triple crown prospects to do herself justice in any of her three finals.' Certainly she played a nervous and ill-judged singles match, losing 11–8, 11–0. The doubles was a much more exciting affair. The Japanese holders, Aizawa and Takenaka (whom Beck and Gilks had beaten in Edinburgh), concentrated at first on trying to play Gillian out of the game, consistently by-passing her at the net. Miss Beck, whose interest in doubles play had only lately been kindled, was forced to be a ball of fire across the back of the court. For whatever reason, Gillian's touch deserted her and the tantalisingly-close match slipped away from England, 15–10, 10–15, 15–11. Gillian's one success was to recapture the mixed title that she had won with Roger Mills four years earlier. She and Derek Talbot were faced by young Nora Gardner and Elliot Stuart, who had easily beaten the holders, Pri and Ulla Strand. At last Gillian came to life, and though they were once 9–15 and 11–13 down, they made it.

The day had started so well for England that by its close there was more disappointment than joy. Nevertheless, for England to have provided five of the ten finalists, and for Gillian to have played in three when not another player was involved in three events beyond the quarter-final stage, were both astonishing achievements.

7 Gold and more gold

It's no surprise that so many badminton players marry badminton players. Most of them devote so much of their lives to the game that they have little chance to meet anybody else. In the course of the story so far we have fallen over no end of shuttlecock weddings: Jane Colman to Martin Boutle, Angela Bairstow to Ian Palmer, Jenny Pritchard to David Horton, Sue Pound to Paul Whetnall, Linda Spencer (once ranked fourth in England) to the Australian doubles champion Donald Cory — and, of course, Gillian Perrin to Mike Gilks. As the 1973–74 season starts, there's a new name at the top of the game: Eva Twedberg, European and twice All-England Champion, has become Eva Stuart, wife of Elliot, the Northumberland player who developed a splendid doubles partnership with Derek Talbot. While we're at it, it would be worth anticipating a few more that are going to continue to occupy space both in badminton and in this book. Margaret Boxall married a South African player, Eddy Allen; Maggie Beck married chairman of selectors Ron Lockwood; Barbara Giles married Ed Sutton; Nora Gardner married Jo Perry; and Ann Forrest, who hasn't appeared yet but plays a critical part later, married Malcolm Statt and then the tall Dane, Steen Stovgaard. Lene Koppen, the delightful Danish dentist, also married in the game, but unlike all the others, she decided she would not change her name.

That is not par for the course for the Danes, two of the most famous of whom — both All-England champions — changed their names quite without matrimonial pressures. Erland Kops, who won seven singles and four doubles titles, achieved his successes after changing from Erland Olsen; Svend Pri won the first of his four titles as Svend Andersen. Sometimes the change seems to do you no badminton good at all. The first Indonesian to win the All-England singles was simply named Tan Joe Hok. Subsequently he became Hendra Kartanagara and disappeared from the roll of honour; and to the great relief of the Press, little was heard of Njoo Kiem Bie after he took on the name of Koesbianto Setdadharmaatmadja. The Press have been known, of course, to inflict their own changes on unsuspecting players. Apart from the Gilks-Gilkes-Jilks-Jelks bit, the Malaysian Oon Chong Hau emerged in the *Telegraph* one morning as Charlie Boon!

All this came up because in October Eva Twedberg played her first tournament in her new name, the Worcestershire Open. The committee almost unbelievably chose her and Maggie Beck as the two seeds in the women's singles and did not name Gillian Gilks, the current All-England runner-up. Gillian responded by beating Mrs Stuart handsomely in the semi-final, 11–0, 11–8 — but she lost even more heavily to Maggie in the final. That was not quite the opening of the season. It began with the first sponsored circuit competition the game had known, the Grandee, which covered four weeks and ten sessions of play, each in a different spot. It involved men's singles only, and only five players were invited to take part: Eddy, Hunt, Stevens, Talbot and Whetnall. Each played two games against every other player twice, giving each man a possible 60 points to record against each of the other four by the end of the circuit, a maximum total of 240. With an MG car as first prize — much the richest reward a British player had ever known — Derek Talbot was inspired. Against such opposition, he recorded the phenomenal total of 233 points. Paul Whetnall took one of their four games off him, and apart from losing one point to Ray Stevens, there was not another tremor in his progress.

The losers didn't do badly: Whetnall went home with a cine kit, Stevens with a portable TV set, Eddy with a stereo record player and Hunt, who beat Eddy but nobody else, with a watch. The women looked on, green-eyed. Off they went next week-end to the prize-less, two-day round-robin at Guildford, the Granwood Invitation Singles, where Margaret Beck registered her third consecutive win. In the final, Gillian won the first four points and never another. Reporting for the *Badminton Gazette*, Dorothy Hinchcliff wrote: 'One felt when watching that perhaps Margaret had gained such ascendancy that Gillian might never beat her again.' But as Mrs Hinchcliff went on to remark, badminton is full of surprises, and a week later Gillian beat her in the final of the West Sussex Open. Gillian won the Wimbledon Open too (in which Eva Stuart beat Maggie Beck) as well as both doubles events in both tournaments.

Gillian played the English Nationals in December with Nora Gardner as doubles partner. They won that event, for Gillian's third consecutive year; she and Talbot won the mixed again (her sixth), but for the third year Miss Beck took the singles. Neither of the leading women contested the London Open, giving Miss Gardner the chance — which she seized with style and delight — to take her most important singles title. Beck and Gilks were together again for the doubles, winning a brilliantly exciting match against Gardner and Sue Whetnall (Miss Boxall was playing with Barbara Giles), and Talbot and Gilks continued their overwhelming progress in the mixed.

All of that was not much more than a warm-up for the two massive events of the season — the greatest season of Gillian's life, so far. At the end of January, the Commonwealth Games in New Zealand, and in April the European championships in Vienna. The seedings for the Commonwealth Games, announced a week before the opening ceremony in Christchurch, reflected the English domination of the sport. Clearly, it was going to be a prestigious domestic matter, at least as far as our women were concerned. The defending men's champion, Canadian Jamie Paulson, was named top singles seed, followed by Talbot and Whetnall; Beck and Gilks headed the women's singles. Beyond Canada and Malaysia, there was no opposition to stand in the way of Britain shovelling the medals in a sack and flying home with them. Indeed, there was nothing much more memorable in the female opposition than the match in a warm-up tournament in which Gillian was facing Jane Youngberg, of Canada. As play was about to begin, Miss Youngberg gasped, giggled and ran to the umpire for permission to leave the court. She had forgotten her knickers.

Alarm struck the English players on the day of the opening ceremony, when Ray Stevens (seeded seventh in the singles) went down with chickenpox. Remarkably, nobody else picked it up and, surprisingly, Stevens recovered in time to play in the doubles with Mike Tredgett. *Times* writer Norman Fox laid his hand nicely on the atmosphere of that opening ceremony:

'The 10th British Commonwealth Games opened here today with 35,500 people watching eight men with lawn mowers cut the grass in the centre of the Queen Elizabeth II Park. Nothing could have symbolised the refreshingly mellow New Zealand character more accurately than that rural sight, after 13 years of planning, political and financial battling, threats of boycotts by African nations and the appalling memories of the tragedy of Munich.'

In an exceedingly chill wind the athletes shivered in the arena as the programme fell peacefully further and further behind schedule. The youngsters forming the colourful 'NZ' symbol found themselves forced, after a long stand, to defect for urgent natural causes, but in due course the £3.3 million Games got under way. For the leading players, the first rounds of the badminton competition are no preparation for the battles to come. Both Margaret Beck and Gillian had byes to the second round, where Maggie won her match 11–1, 11–1 and Mrs Yasmin Kanji of Tanzania failed to win a point off Gillian. Mrs Joan Jones of Australia fared little better in the third round and of the four semi-finalists only Sue Whetnall had lost a game. Gillian then lost one, as usual, to the Malaysian, Sylvia Ng (who married her partner's brother and became Sylvia Ang), but Beck swept Mrs Whetnall aside 11–1, 11–9 to set up a repeat of the 1970 Commonwealth Games final.

On the men's side, Derek Talbot had a splendid semi-final against the eventual champion, Punch Gunalan of Malaysia, who won 15–11 in the third; and Paul Whetnall lost heavily to the holder, Paulson, in a match in the course of which he damaged a tendon. He was unable to contest the bronze medal with Talbot, and also had to pull out of the mixed doubles final. This he and Nora Gardner had reached after a pulsating semi against Elliot Stuart and Sue Whetnall (who took the bronze). Talbot and Gillian, who had never been stretched, thus had a disappointing walk-over to the gold medal. The women's final, as expected, saw Maggie and Gillian challenging the holders, Boxall and Whetnall, and beating them easily. By then, of course, the women's singles had been decided.

The two girls, who even then were only 22 and 23 years old, had played so many disappointing matches against each other over the previous four or five years that it was no surprise when this turned out to be another. 'At this time,' said Gillian, 'we both had the same coach (Jake Downey) and were playing the same style of game year in and year out. We each knew everything the other was going to do, and we desperately needed a new approach to the game. This match in Christchurch wasn't too bad, but it wasn't particularly brilliant — we both made far too many mistakes for that. When two players are as level as we used to be, there is always just about the same chance (whatever the seeding may be) for either of us to produce something a bit extra on the day that will do the trick.'

On that day, January 31st, 1974, Miss Beck got away to a cracking start, 8–0, and an icy hand descended on the Gilks supporters. They had seen all this before. Then, unexpectedly, Gillian dug in, kept cool, got the shuttle back and watched Maggie hit it out. ('You never throw a game away in singles, it's all too short. It's worth fighting for every point to the end.') The younger girl seemed first to become complacent and then to lose her concentration completely. She didn't win another point in the opening game. Gilks went straight on in the same vein to lead 6–1 in the second, and then it was Maggie's turn to fight back to 8–8. That was a critically testing moment for Gillian and she survived it, clearing to a beautiful length and maintaining her overhead dominance. It was, as they say, ding-dong all the way — at one period service changed hands eight times without the point being won — but though it was exciting for the crowd, it was not good badminton. At last, at 8–10 (match point) Maggie put a smash out and Gillian had won her first major international singles title, beating the Commonwealth Games and All-England champion. By the end of the evening she had collected three gold medals, a phenomenal and unique achievement in badminton. At last, wrote *The Guardian* correspondent, Gillian Gilks proved that she has the staying power to match her beautiful array of strokes.

Every one of the 10 members of the English team won at least a gold or a silver medal, and altogether they took 17 of the possible 20 golds. 'Gillian is the pride of Steyning' trumpeted the local paper back home (Mike Gilks, who was at Christchurch as an umpire, had moved down to Sussex with his job the previous summer), and suddenly she was the girl of the moment. The Steyning Cricket Club made her their first female honorary life member and added to her silver collection with a salver. The local hotel put on a slap-up dinner for her, and the parish council weighed in with a water colour of Old Steyning. Whenever anyone wanted a fête opened, Gillian was trundled along. Cheers and bouquets and speeches — and however kind and generous they all were, it doesn't take long to have enough of all that. Besides, it was now February and there were other things to think about: in March, the All-England again; in April, the European championships. Now that Gillian Gilks had at last forsaken the practice of always being the bridesmaid, who was going to lay the odds against her being the star turn at those weddings too?

She was still only 23 years old and she faced her tenth All-England Championships. It was weird, almost unreal. For five years, you remember, she was put out in the first round of the singles (or at least her first match, if she happened to draw a bye). In 1973 she had reached the final of all three events and won the mixed with Talbot. In 1974 she was a triple finalist again, an historic achievement: it was her fifth consecutive women's doubles final and her fourth consecutive mixed — the fifth in six years.

Following her on court at Wembley, Rudy Hartono was about to win his seventh singles title in succession. He had already caused some consternation by conceding a game to Hansen, of Denmark, only the second Hartono had lost in all his years in these championships. In the semi-final Sture Johnsson, of Sweden, took another off him, and in the final he had a tremendous battle with Punch Gunalan — 8–15, 15–9, 15–10. Those seven titles equalled the record of his predecessor, Erland Kops. The Kops wins were spread over ten years, but, as he was fond of saying (but quietly), he earned all his. International badminton players have never been happy at what they regard as the Indonesian tendency to agree on the result before a match takes place, if it is between two or four of their own countrymen. Regardless of that, Hartono may well have been the greatest singles player ever seen (he hardly ever played doubles). He had a marvellously placid temperament and was beautiful to watch. As Gillian Gilks so aptly put it, because he was almost faultless, there seemed nothing outstanding about his play. He just didn't make mistakes. Not a very talkative character, certainly not when he was in England, he was no doubt getting pretty tired of having to make the winner's speech at the championships dinner every year. Indeed, he gave the impression of pulling the same piece of paper out of his pocket each year, with a few words substituted here and there.

The whole Indonesian approach to badminton was quite unlike anything with which British players were familiar. The extended family system is very strong in their country, and one often had the feeling that their badminton teams abroad were just such a family. The players were always together, always taking care of each other and giving the impression of absolute friendliness. Badminton is, without doubt, the national sport of Indonesia and the one from which the nation gains the greatest international prestige. Because of this, the rich section of the community — and theirs is largely a community without a middle class — pour money into badminton and enable the poor to live a heroic life, if they are good badminton players. Hero worship of the male players is immense. After Liem Swie King had won his second All-England singles crown in 1979, a local benefactor had a life-size statue of him erected in his home town. In 1980, it was taken down: King was beaten in China. The men are treated like film stars, and sometimes become film stars when they cease playing. They couldn't do the two together, as a top-class player in Indonesia is expected to train for up to six hours a day for 11 months of the year.

It is a nation, like many of the East, in which women take second place. Badminton, to some extent, can override that; but it would not be in the Indonesian character for a woman to choose badminton rather than domesticity, or to be allowed to exercise her talents at the game after marriage. The brilliant Minarni deserved far more entries on the All-England roll of honour than her one doubles win with Miss Koestijah in 1968, and it is an unrealistic representation of the all-round strength of Indonesian badminton that until 1979 those were the only female names from that country ever to win an All-England title.

In these championships of 1974, there were no Indonesian women competitors at all — despite the fact that they had reached the final of the Uber Cup, where Minarni had so easily beaten Hiroe Yuki. Miss Yuki devastated Maggie Beck in the quarter-final and reached the final with a three-setter against Joke van Beusekom. In the other half of the draw, Gillian Gilks was in great shape, marching through former champion Takenaka and future champion Koppen (who had twice beaten Miss Beck in the run-up to the All-England) to face Hiroe Yuki, who had won the title five years earlier. As the Press had it, Gillian played three times as many winners as Miss Yuki, but was 100 per cent worse off in the tally of errors.

'When you're a stroke player, like me, you've got far more potential winners to play, and you must play them; but you are also likely to be far more inaccurate. A safe player like Lene Koppen, a runner, will make far fewer winners and far fewer mistakes. Against her, if you're not careful, you beat yourself. Yuki has a bit of everything. She has strokes and she uses them very soundly; she is a good all-round player with good physique, a good runner, a good temperament, a good champion — there's very little you can fault her on. Any time you beat her, you've done well. I reckon possibly the greatest match I ever played was when I beat her in the All-England semis of 1978.'

In 1974, Yuki's discipline and consistency carried the day 11–6, 12–11, though Gillian reached game point in the second at 10–9. Then she and Maggie Beck captured the doubles title for the first time, beating Boxall and Whetnall handsomely, but there was another disappointment awaiting Gillian in the mixed final, for which she and Derek Talbot were strongly fancied to retain their title against the unexpected challenge of Dave Eddy and Sue Whetnall.

'We thought Dave would eventually give way, but he didn't. He was a hot and cold player, but that day he was really hot. We kept plugging away to try and find the chink in his armour, but he wouldn't let us get there and they took us 15–10 in the third.'

Still, three Commonwealth golds and three All-England finals with one gold wasn't bad going for one season. And though the climax of the season was past, there were still two huge events to come: the European championships and the first tour of China by an English team; and on the side, a week before Vienna, Surrey were attempting to win the county championship for the tenth successive year. The final was on Essex's home ground at Redbridge and it could not have been a closer contest: Surrey made it by nine matches to eight, with eight of the 17 going to three games. Gillian won all four of hers, including an 11–2, 11–2 thrashing of Nora Gardner and an unexpected win in straight games by Keith Andrews and Gillian over the international Essex pair of Ray Stevens and Miss Gardner. One of her doubles with Angela (Bairstow) Palmer, however, against Miss Gardner and Barbara Giles was a real cracker: 9–15, 15–8, 17–16.

In the process of helping to retain the European team championship, Gillian did not drop one of her seven matches, though on the last day Lene Koppen held match point against her in the second game. Four days later, Gillian had made history again: the first player ever to win three European titles. It really was an astonishing golden treble, in the course of which she did not lose one game of singles. 'This must establish her,' wrote Dicky Rutnagur in the *Telegraph*, 'as one of the greatest women players of all time.' Even Miss Koppen was no trouble in the singles final: 11–6, 11–5. In the women's doubles, Gillian and Maggie beat Sue Whetnall and Nora Gardner 15–10, 15–11 (Margaret Boxall, to almost everyone's surprise, had been left out of the team); and in the mixed Gilks and Talbot dropped the first game but easily won the next two against Elliot Stuart and Mrs Whetnall.

Gillian's trip to the title was such a smooth one, requiring no obviously heroic effort, just consistently superb badminton, that it seemed to be accepted at the time without the honour due to it. There were, indeed, more remarkable matches elsewhere. Derek Talbot's defeat of the men's singles champion, Svend Pri, 15–9, 7–15, 15–2, certainly raised more eyebrows (particularly when Derek's shorts split as he leapt to avoid a smash), and Lene Koppen's victory over the holder, Maggie Beck, in the semi-finals was sensational. After losing the first game 11–6, the Briton went downhill even more rapidly in the second, till she stood on the brink of humiliation at 1–10 — match point. Her Cumberland resolution then, without warning, transformed her and she won the game 12–10 and stormed on to lead 7–3 in the third. At the moment when it looked as though we were surely heading for a repeat of the Commonwealth Games final, Miss Beck crumbled to dust and won not another point. As she said shortly before leaving for China, she had gone through a long bad patch — or at least, she hoped she was through it: 'There's always a lot of pressure on you when you've won lots of things before. Now I have the chance to do well in China, and I'm really looking forward to it. Nobody's unbeatable, nobody.'

Well, nobody but the Chinese, perhaps. In front of 18,000 spectators in Peking on May 4th, England lost their first international by six matches to one. Even Gillian and Maggie couldn't pull out a win in the doubles; it was only Gillian and Derek Talbot who avoided the whitewash, winning the mixed in two games. Their programme over the three weeks encompassed two encounters with the People's Republic of China (unofficial internationals, as that part of China was not a member of the International Badminton Federation), one with a 'China Select' team and four with provinces or groups of provinces. Everywhere they went, it was 'friendship first, competition second,' but nevertheless the Chinese never lost. Just as they had demonstrated during their tour of England two years earlier, their fitness and speed were so outstanding that equality of talent, where it existed, became of secondary importance.

Margaret Beck believed the British girls were as fit as the Chinese, and that the

In the garden at Steyning after bringing home three gold medals from the 1974 Commonwealth Games in New Zealand

Hilarity in the camp as England's women pick up tips before leaving on the first badminton tour of China. From the left: Heather Nielsen, Nora Gardner, Maggie Beck, Chai Lee Wong, Gillian, Sue Whetnall, Margaret Boxall

difference between them was the speed with which they reached the shuttle and the calmness with which they played even when under the greatest pressure (some would say that superior fitness can lead a player to both these advantages). Nora Gardner remembered them for their competitiveness, their determination never to give up. Elliot Stuart said that, as well as being extremely fit and agile, and possessing lightningly-fast reflexes, the three leading Chinese men had the ability to play almost any shot from any position on the court. If Stuart is right, there is nothing more to be said. Certainly the results bear him out: the Chinese won all eleven men's singles played on the tour, and eight of the eleven doubles.

As expected, the girls' record was slightly better, and their most disappointing element was the Beck and Gilks partnership, who won only one of their five doubles (other women's doubles partnerships won six of eight matches). Only Maggie and Gillian contested the singles, Gillian winning one of four and Maggie two of six. 'Victory is transitory,' declaimed one of their hosts at the very first reception, 'but the friendships made go on for ever.' Nevertheless, the ease with which the Chinese swept aside two of the best six players in the rest of the world must have given them considerable satisfaction.

Incidentally, two Asian journalists trying to discover the secret of Chinese success came up with some interesting details in the *Bangkok Post* early in 1974. Researching the backgrounds of the leading Chinese players, they found that many of them came from Indonesia — a fact, if it is true, that clashes severely with the official Chinese biographies. The top male players who took part in the tour of Britain in 1973, and in the British tour of China in 1974, were said to be Hou Chia-Chang (born in Kwangtung, 1942), Tang Hsien-hu (born in Kwangtung, 1942), Fang Kai-hsiang (born Fukien, 1940) and Chen Tien-hsiang (born Gukien, 1940). The *Bangkok Post* newshounds don't agree: Hou used to be called Houw Ka Tjong and was champion of Central Java before he emigrated to China; Tang came from Jakarta and actually played for Indonesia under the name of Thing Hian Houw; Fang used to have the much merrier name of Hong Gay Siong and came from East Java; and Chen was from Solo, Central Java.

The lady who proved so devastating in Britain was Miss Chen Yu-niang, then the national singles and doubles champion. She too, apparently, was Indonesian by birth, where she was Tan Giok Nio; Liang Chiu-hsia, who was unbeatable on the tour of China, was an Indonesian Uber Cup trialist in 1966, according to the *Bangkok Post* boys, and was the eldest sister of the famous men's doubles champion, Tjun Tjun. All quite fascinating, but which version is fact and which fiction is likely to remain a mystery to Westerners. It was hard enough, in Peking, to decide whether you were playing Chen Tien-hsiang or Cheng Chin-chin, and whether there was a difference between Liu Hsia and Liang Chiu-hsia.

Anyway, wherever they came from, it was an immensely successful and happy tour, played in front of huge crowds who, though always orderly (unlike the Indonesians), seemed ecstatically happy and bursting with appreciation for both sides. Gillian's lasting memory of the trip is of people — unending masses of people everywhere, in the badminton halls, the buses, the shops, on the pavements, on bicycles. She remembers too the occasional boredom: 'When you had practised and eaten and seen the Great Wall, there wasn't a lot to do. One empty evening we insisted that our guide let us go for a walk. It was a hard job, but in the end he gave in. He took us for a walk — 100 yards down the road and back again.'

Mike Tredgett remembers the impeccable politeness of the people and their everlasting courtesy. Tom Marrs, an official with the party, brought away a thought that clung to many of us who were in Moscow in 1980: that however alarmed the British might be with the restricted way of life in these countries, it was clear that the older people who lived there knew life was much better now than it used to be before the revolution, or the liberation, and that the younger people who had known no other way of life were quite happy with their lot: 'During our stay, at no time were we subjected to political propaganda. My over-riding impression was that, although the Chinese obviously believe their system is the right one for them in their circumstances, they are making no great attempt to impose it on others.'

He also recalled hilariously, in the *Badminton Gazette*, that the stunning honesty of the Chinese people, and their care for their guests, made it almost impossible to dispose of unwanted items, even in waste baskets, since the contents would frequently be sifted and returned to the owners. On one occasion, as the party waited to board their coach after an official visit, the guide announced that a one-cent coin (about a fifth of a penny) had been found in the coach. It was imperative that the owner was traced. When it became clear that the coach was not going to move until ownership was established, Elliot Stuart volunteered and collected the coin. As the coach moved off through the crowds of children, he tossed it out of the window. Back at the hotel later that day, the guide arrived triumphantly with the coin: a small boy had spotted it and had traced the coach back to the hotel.

As the long season and the summer faded, and even the fête-opening abated, the autumn season of more serious celebration arrived. Gillian's seven Commonwealth and European gold medals, and her three All-England finals, put her at least in line for the Sportswoman of the Year awards. At the highest national level, there are three of these: the *Daily Express* conducts a readers' poll and presents trophies to the man and woman they choose; BBC Television invite viewers to name their sports personality of the year and get a massive response, which culminates in the long and frequently fascinating sports review of the year programme and presentation on the air of their trophy; and the Sports Writers' Association invite their own 400 members to take part in a much more detailed and professional poll. This reflects not public popularity, but the writers' view of pure achievement. They are asked to vote for the man and the woman who have done most to increase Britain's sporting prestige internationally. It lacks the glamour of the BBC presentation, but it is the award that the recipients usually hold most dear, because it is given by people who (loosely speaking) know what they are talking about. In 1974 the two winners were

John Conteh, the world light-heavyweight champion, and Gillian Gilks — neither of whom won either of the other awards.

John Conteh must have been slightly puzzled to find himself only fourth in the *Express* poll after winning all the titles open to him, but then there's no accounting for readers' tastes: in 1972 they voted Gordon Banks sportsman of the year after his tragic accident, not Richard Meade, who won three gold medals at the Munich Olympics; and in 1970 their female winner was Lillian Board, whom everybody loved but who had not taken part in the Commonwealth Games at all. Never mind, viewers are just as dotty: back in 1954 the BBC TV nomination was not Roger Bannister, who had run the sub-four-minute mile, but Chris Chataway, who was one of his pace-makers. And in 1970 it was not Tony Jacklin, who had just achieved golfing immortality by holding the British and US Open titles at the same time, but dear old Henry Cooper, who had yet again successfully defended his boxing titles against Jack Bodell. But mention of Henry Cooper casts a curious light on the SWA poll, come to think of it: in 1966 he put Cassius Clay on his back and in 1968 he won the European heavyweight title, but in neither year — nor in any other — did he ever find a place even among the top six of their sportsmen of the year.

Anyway, in 1974 the sports writers seemed to get it dead right, and Gillian Gilks became the first badminton player of either sex not just to have won the SWA award, but even to have reached the top six in the voting — and the awards go back to 1950. 'It was a marvellous compliment to win it,' said Gillian, 'not just for me, but for the sport. It's very flattering to get any kind of award, but that one seems to me the greatest of the lot. Coming on top of the Commonwealth and the Europeans, it made 1974 quite a year to remember.'

8 Disaster and discontent

Injuries in badminton are generally confined to the sort of aggravating pulls and strains and twists that are an ever-present hazard in a game that calls for so many sudden, darting changes of direction. Gillian Gilks opened the 1974–5 season with a notably annoying one: demonstrating receipt of service at a coaching clinic towards the end of September, she leaped backwards on to her left foot and tore the ligaments in the ankle. The leg was put into plaster at Middlesex Hospital from toes to knee and she had to pull out immediately from the Hearts of Oak invitation singles tournament that was about to take place at Reading. She also missed the Surrey Closed, the Worcestershire and Wimbledon Opens and, worst of all, the second world invitation tournament in Jakarta.

Though this came rather too early in the season to catch British players at their best (particularly after such a long and hard season as the previous one), it would have been difficult to catch Margaret Beck any better. Thirsting for an important victory after losing all her international titles the previous season, she managed a triumph, beating Hiroe Yuki in the semi and Tati Sumirah (Indonesia) in the final without losing a game to either of them. Before 18,000 wildly excited spectators and in almost unbearable heat and humidity, it was a superb effort. No other Briton reached a final, though Margaret Boxall and Mrs Whetnall were in the semi-finals of both the women's and the mixed doubles, with Paul Whetnall and Derek Talbot.

In the absence of Gillian, Heather Nielsen (also injured) and Nora Gardner, the Hearts of Oak went almost unchallenged to Margaret Beck (her fourth successive win in the invitation singles). It did, however, throw up one or two interesting results along the way. Neither Anne Statt (formerly Forrest) nor Jane Webster, both nationally ranked at seven and eight, managed to win their groups; and 14-year-old Karen Bridge, though not statistically successful, made a remarkable impression on some of her adult opponents in her first appearance at this level.

Gillian didn't play again until she made a rather tentative appearance in the Oxfordshire championships in the second week of November — probably the longest break from badminton ever forced on her. There is no way you can rush leg injuries into healing themselves, and no way you can pretend it will be all right when it isn't. With a contact injury, you can grin and bear it. Badminton players often get a crack in the hand or on the back of the leg caused by both players in a doubles going for the shuttle that falls between them, and a few noses have been broken by the racket of the partner flashing overhead as he comes back from the net. You feel rather more foolish when you hit yourself in the face, as Gillian did a year later when she was playing a doubles with Sue Whetnall at Wimbledon. Whipping one of Maggie Beck's smashes off the floor, Gillian's follow through went straight to her cheek, steel on bone. Very nasty at the time, but no lasting damage; in fact, she was soon afterwards modelling a track suit on television for the CCPR with both eyes a rare shade and plastered in make-up.

She took the Oxfordshire very gently, losing the final to the up-and-coming Paula Kilvington and going out in the second match of the doubles to Miss Kilvington and Karen Bridge. Indeed, though Gillian was playing again remarkably soon after the injury, it clearly affected her for the rest of the year. She did not win another singles title until January 1975 — by which time Margaret Beck was *hors de combat* with a broken bone in her foot. Her win was at Crawley, in the third and last of the Hearts of Oak circuit. Quite separate from the invitation singles that opened the season, this circuit comprised the Northern, the English Nationals and the Sussex Open, the points won at these three tournaments determining which players went on to the Hearts of Oak finals in Manchester at the end of January. With Maggie only just back in time for the finals, Gillian lifted all three titles.

By then she had been off on a swift ten-man, three-match tour in Japan that went extraordinarily well for the English, who lost the first 3–2 and won both the others 5–0. It was a toss-up whether that would leave her razor-sharp for the Hearts of Oak, or blunt with jet-lag. It certainly didn't seem to do her any harm, though a fully-mobile Maggie Beck would no doubt have made the day much more difficult. It was a more important day than it seemed, for from January 1st there were far-reaching changes in the regulations governing amateur status. The old £10 prize limit was scrapped, and those who registered with the BAE as 'tournament players' could collect cash up to the IBF limit of £100 — not just 'gift tokens'. The same players were from that time allowed to accept advertising or other commercial contracts, providing the BAE approved of them, and also 'broken time' payments.

The move was long overdue, but nevertheless it was made sensibly and in time to prevent too much abuse of the amateur regulations that had so far pertained. And it enabled the Hearts of Oak Society to put up a total of £1,769 for their four-tournament circuit, £750 of which was at stake in the finals. With £100 for her singles title and £50 for each of the doubles, Gillian moved off with the richest prize ever offered in badminton. It seems modest enough now, with £23,500 being offered at the Friends' Provident Masters tournament at the Albert Hall in 1980 (£3,000 for each singles winner alone), but even in 1975 it was a significant breakthrough in the emergence of badminton from its dainty, and quite misleading, image. No doubt about it, with the prize money that is now offered in badminton, and the amount of sponsorship the BAE has attracted in recent years, it is now possible for the outstanding players of the country to earn a very good living. For obvious reasons, precise contract figures are hard to come by, but players of real world class would now reckon to earn £20,000 outside prize money. This would be for using the rackets of one firm and the clothing of another, and guaranteeing not to use any other; for appearing in their advertisements and public relations functions, and perhaps for attending a sales conference now and then.

The leading badminton players, like the leading tennis players, now have managers to look after their commercial interests and to get the best deal possible for them. When a contract is nearing its end, the manager will sniff around the rival firms to see how much they are prepared to pay the player to change rackets or shoes or whatever. On the side come little benefits like tournament entry fees and travel expenses being paid, and perhaps a car being provided that ostentatiously declares 'Gillian Gilks drives a Zombie provided by Spare Cars Ltd.' To maintain such status, the player has of course to maintain her standards and to be seen to be successful in a large number of tournaments — preferably on television. The BAE's rules, like those of the Lawn Tennis Association, are very strict about the wearing of promotional emblems on clothing on court. You may remember tennis champion Ann Jones, a long time ago, being in trouble for carrying a bag on a Wimbledon court that clearly proclaimed the name of its provider. Gillian was in similar trouble after the Hearts of Oak final at Crystal Palace in 1977. During the warm-up the shuttles were found to be the wrong speed and a fresh supply had to be produced. While she was waiting for them, Gillian kept warm by wearing her tracksuit top, with 'Sondico' written across the back. Nobody, she said, spoke to her about it at the time, or she would have left the court, or turned the jacket inside out; but afterwards the wrath of the BAE descended on her for exceeding the permitted two-inch emblem on her court wear. In other lands, there are other rules — in Denmark, for instance, you can play in slogans. But not in England. Not yet.

So, where were we? Taking £200 home after the Hearts of Oak in January, 1975. Then there was a quick Uber Cup European semi-final win over Holland and the Dutch Open singles title for Gillian before another minor disaster at home. Influenza struck Gillian during the Surrey Open at Wimbledon, by which time she had reached two finals and was heading for the third. Of greater concern to England was the fact that only 10 days remained before the Uber zone final against Denmark. She made it, and though she and Heather Nielsen both lost their singles (Gilks to Koppen, 11–6, 11–3), the other five matches were won and tickets were booked for a trip to Indonesia in the summer.

The All-England was full of surprises and not many of them were nice ones. Hiroe Yuki, the holder, and Lene Koppen were seeded one and two, Maggie Beck and Gillian three and four. With a brilliant display, Gillian reached her third consecutive final by beating Miss Koppen 11–3, 11–7 in the semi; at 36, Heather Nielsen surprisingly reached the quarter-finals; and at 20, Nora Gardner won her first All-England championship, the mixed with Elliot Stuart; but that was about the end of

Two of the men in her life: Mike Gilks, Gillian's former badminton-umpiring husband; and (below) *Derek Talbot, the classic mixed doubles partner with whom she won three European and three All-England titles. Centre is Badminton Association of England president Stuart Wyatt, after presenting their fourth English National trophy in 1975*

Gillian Gilks

The legs that have electrified spectators all the way round the world

the good news. Paul Whetnall, the first Englishman to be seeded at the All-England for 28 years, failed to reach his appointed position (Svend Pri won the title, ending Hartono's magnificent run); Miss Beck was beaten in the quarters by Hartono's sister, the unseeded Utami Dewi; there were no Englishmen in the doubles semis and neither of the women's doubles top seeds, Beck-Gilks and Boxall-Whetnall, reached the final. Cap that with the fact that Gillian once more failed at the final hurdle, after a notably nervous start, and that she did not contest the mixed at all, and you have a considerable package of disappointment. The mixed affair was particularly aggravating, for Derek Talbot and Gillian had never lost to either of the eventual finalists, Stuart and Gardner and the German pair, Maywald and Steden. With Talbot at first doubtful about playing in the mixed at all, Gillian asked the BAE to enter her with the Dane, Svend Pri. The Association decided not to accept that entry because of the mixed nationality; but subsequently accepted the entry of Talbot with another Dane, Ulla Strand. Though an isolated incident, it seems to have been the first step on Gillian's apparently endless escalator of trouble with the establishment and its officials — and another was close at hand. Anyway, the result of it all was a headline in the Press that said: 'Mrs Gilks fails in another final.' Understandably, it did not say 'Mrs Gilks again proves herself second best badminton player in the world.' Understandable, that is, to anyone who works for a newspaper; not always so clear to the player concerned.

Despite another win for Hiroe Yuki at Wembley, the English Uber Cup team went to Jakarta at the end of May with considerable confidence. Both Beck and Gilks seemed to have recovered from their leg injuries, and England's chances of at least beating Indonesia, to meet Japan in the final, were thoroughly good. Jane Webster, the 1974 All-England junior champion, was taken as third singles player, with Barbara Giles as the reserve to the established doubles pair of Boxall and Whetnall. They stopped in Kuala Lumpur on the way for a warm-up friendly against Malaysia, the first international ever played against that nation, in which Margaret Boxall did not play but England won 7–0. Nor was 'Great Margaret' fit enough to play in the practices in Jakarta, but nevertheless the selectors (team captain Ron Lockwood and coach Jake Downey) restored her to the team for the vital match against Indonesia. Unable to decide whether to play Beck or Gilks as number one in the singles, Lockwood tossed a coin for it and played Beck. She lost to Tati Sumirah, Gillian beat Theresia Widiastuty, and Jane Webster was annihilated by Utami Dewi. The reporting of these opening games in the *Indonesia Times* — where badminton is a major interest — deserves reading in full. This is the English-language newspaper of a country in which English is, quite plainly, not developed to perfection:

> 'Under the roar of a well crowded stadium Tati Sumirah surprisingly defeated All-England champion Margaret Beck at Senayan Sports Hall yesterday night. Tati was very nervous in the first set, her dropshots were while and seldom crossed over the net. Her main weakness war for her backhand.
>
> On the other-hand, Margaret Beck played beautifully in this set. Her dropshot

were almost perfect. Her poise was calm and could easily return any difficult shot. Soon she was leading 5–2. Tati Sumirah bettered her play and started catching up with her loobing. The score became six all and seven all. But the first set ended 7–11 for Beck.

After the first set, Margaret Beck outplayed herself and became very tired. She lost the second set 7–11.

Only for times, the shuttlecock changed hand on the rubber set. Margaret Beck first led 5–0, then Tati changed the scored to 7–5. After this, Margaret Beck was very tired and the third set ended in eight minutes, 11–6 for Tati Sumirah.

With this interesting attitude Theresia Widiastuti led Gillian Gilks to rubber set, after the first set was won by Gilks. As usual, the Indonesian was not well geared until score was half way, but it was too late for Tuti to catch up. She never went beyond five points in the first set.

On the second set Miss Gilks was already influenced by Miss Widiastuti's attitude. This set Miss Tuti led the score all the way until the score was deuce, 9–9. Theresia won all the three points ending the game 12–9.

On the third set, Theresia led the game again 8–7. After this point she was very tired and beaten 8–11.

On the third singles between Utami Dewi and Jane Webster the Indonesian first ranking was no match for the English. The first set Dewi won 11–6, the second set 11–0.

In the doubles Indonesia's Minarni/Regina Masli played Beck/Gillian Gilks. But the result was still not known yet for this news had to go to the printing house immediately.'

The delightful naivety of the last sentence was frequently seen in the reporting of evening events, in contrast to the frantic efforts of British reporters on such occasions to cover up the fact that the beastly event was staged so late — as is so often the case in badminton — that they couldn't meet the deadline. Incidentally, apart from being televised, the tie received a 'shuttle by shuttle' commentary on radio from the moment it began to the last point at 12.50 a.m. It was a day later before the *Indonesian Times* could pass on to its readers the dramatic news about the four doubles matches on which the whole rubber depended. Going into them 1–2 down, England levelled with a Beck-Gilks win over Minarni-Masli, but Boxall and Whetnall narrowly lost their first doubles, to Wiguna and Widiastuti. When the same Indonesia pair faced Beck and Gilks, Indonesia took the first game 15–11 and, as the *Indonesia Times* had it, 'left the crowd gratefully happy.' In the second they roared away to a 10–2 lead before the English girls could dig in; when they did, it was to tremendous effect, taking the game to 13–13 and winning all five points in the setting. England's hopes of challenging Japan then all depended on Beck and Gilks winning the final game, and the pattern of the play must have sent the spectators into a frenzy: Indonesia led 10–1, England led 11–10, 'but the English were already out of breath' and Indonesia won 15–11. The final and meaningless match was won

A sight that few spectators see: Wembley Arena early in the All-England week, with seven courts in action. At the end of the 1975 week, Gillian was runner-up for the second successive year to Hiroe Yuki (Japan)

Paul Whetnall, seen here with Gillian in 1975, was one of the outstanding British singles players of the past 20 years

with appalling ease by Indonesia against Boxall and Whetnall, 15–2, 15–1.

It was, said Gillian, a disastrous evening and one that should not have been allowed to develop as it did. Neither the Japanese nor the Indonesians themselves expected England to be beaten. Two days later the star sports columnist of our favourite paper added his profound comments to the situation:

'The victory of Indonesia was said to be a very appreciated surprise, and well, I don't think I can write much about these events, as I didn't have the opportunity to attend the events (because of football, of course). But I will try to attend the finals: Indonesia — Japan. And I will tell you about it by next week (although you will may be get the results already today — Saturday).'

As you might expect, the badminton reporter was once more frustrated by the lateness of the hour, his account finishing with the words: 'No further results of the other doubles match were learned due to this news had to go to the printing house.' At that time the score was 2–2, but Japan won all the other doubles. But by then English-speaking readers had been treated to an account of the opening singles that would test the prowess of a professor of pidgin English:

'One more Tati Sumirah repeated for her brilliant performance against the Japanese University's Student Champion Atsuko Tokuda in straight set which two days ago she had crumbled fortress of English badminton supremacy.

For relax countenance, coupled with ecstatic dropshots and line drives forced Atsuko to submit to her tempo. Only after three points, the Japanese was already exhausted. Tati kept the manuoevre all the way, never letting Atsuko one point behind.

Duece was reached only once at five all. But this was the last time Atsuko was anywhere near Tati. After 8–5 Atsuko's performance was untidy due to tiredness. The Japanese was lost the first set in high spirit, 5–11. The second set was no difference although Atsuko was full of fight, there was no more tactness in her play. The game ended 11–2 for Tati.'

What we would give to be able to read the next day's paper for Indonesia astonished themselves and their opponents by winning the tie 5–2; alas, no further copies of the *Indonesia Times* reached these shores. We have only the entirely reliable report of the International Badminton Federation secretary, Herbert Scheele (referred to by the local paper throughout the competition as Sir Herbert Scheele) who wrote in *World Badminton* of 'utter pandemonium' breaking out in the huge stadium when Indonesia for the first time captured the Uber Cup. It was he also who wrote this of the tie against England:

'All the Indonesian players performed extremely well, but the same could not be said of their opponents, amongst whom only Mrs Gilks displayed in any degree of consistency their normal high standard of play. One fancies that the many days of waiting to play, whilst watching the three preceding ties, had had its ill effect. Except for Mrs Gilks, they all seemed to lack that very necessary spirit of "raring to go".'

It was indeed a sad time for England, who had never had a better chance of winning the Uber Cup. Nobody could have been unhappier than Maggie Beck that, on that crucial night, she played both singles and doubles like a shadow of her real self — still troubled, apparently, by the injured foot.

In September the team returned to Kuala Lumpur for the third invitation world tournament, for which the girls were joined by Derek Talbot, but not by Elliot Stuart, forcing Talbot to withdraw from the doubles. The first two such championships had been held in Jakarta (the first for men only), and were not regarded by the players — certainly the European players — as having anything like the status of the All-England tournament. In 1974, Svend Pri and Margaret Beck had won the singles, and all the doubles had gone to Indonesians. Again in 1975 the Indonesian men dominated play, but not before there had been the most awful row between Indonesia and the host nation, Malaysia, over the draw.

The men's singles was redrawn on the Monday, following the withdrawal from the tournament of two of the eight seeds, Rudy Hartono and Sture Johnsson (Sweden). They had been in the bottom half of the draw with Flemming Delfs and Liem Swie King, the brilliant Indonesian teenager; in the upper half were Pri, Elo Hansen (Denmark), Bandid Jaiyen (Thailand) and Tjun Tjun, of Indonesia. With the redraw, Tjun Tjun was moved into Hartono's place as second seed and two Malaysians came into seeded positions — but Swie King remained in Tjun Tjun's half. This was the bone of contention, and the All-Indonesia Badminton Federation lodged a strong protest, on the grounds that the IBF regulations state: 'Any two entries from any country which shall be seeded shall be drawn in two separate halves of the draw.' Their immediate reaction was to withdraw from the entire tournament, but after a phone call back home agreed to play on, reluctantly.

The extent of their reluctance was soon apparent. On the Wednesday they withdrew Wahjudi and Christian from the singles, so they could concentrate on doubles; and at the same time requested the organising committee to change the places in the draw of Delfs, the new third seed, and Swie King. When that request was refused, on the day the tournament was to begin, they withdrew Tjun Tjun as well, leaving Swie King as the only Indonesian representative in the singles and removing his strongest opponent. The outcome of all this Indonesian movement, as well as the non-appearance of Stuart, one Dane and two Hong Kong players whose entry permits had been held up, was that seven of the sixteen first round matches were walk-overs. Two of the eight men's doubles were also called off, two of the women's doubles and five of the eight mixed doubles. Three of the mixed defections were Indonesian and one was that of the top seeds, Stuart and Nora Gardner. Maggie Beck, who had entered the mixed with Fleming Delfs, withdrew in favour of Miss Gardner, but she and Delfs lost in the first round to the holders, Christian and Masli of Indonesia, who did not drop a game in retaining their title — not even to Talbot and Gilks.

The four women's singles seeds were Yuki, Beck, Gilks and Sumirah, who all had only two matches to play to reach the semi-finals. The only match in the whole draw to go to three games was Sumirah's surprising win over Miss Beck, 5–11, 11–5, 11–4, to take her to a one-sided final won by Hiroe Yuki. The only other title not taken by Indonesia was the women's doubles, comfortably won by Gilks and Beck. Svend Pri's attempt to retain his singles title ended tragically during his semi with Delfs, when Pri tore a hamstring. The damage to badminton in the East was even greater, thanks to Malaysia's mishandling of the draw. As one of their own journalists put it in the *New Straits Times*, 'The trust and friendship we lost will be hard to regain.' Beyond that, he said, the subsequent Indonesian withdrawals 'only helped to turn the tournament into a bigger bore than had earlier been expected.' One of his colleagues attacked the Badminton Association of Malaysia's 'over-riding mercenary motivation' in charging astronomical admission rates to a tournament that hardly justified its label.

It had, all in all, been a hell of a summer and a hell of a long season during which Gillian first passed her 50th 'cap' for England and later overtook the record of 53 set by Iris Rogers, with whom Gillian had played her first international. But the season had not been all smiles. Spikes of discontent had emerged in the very top rank of the game. Before the new season began, with the English Invitation Singles coming only a month after the World Invitation, two quite shattering decisions were made: the BAE sacked Roger Mills as chief coach, on the grounds that he had contravened his terms of employment by entering into certain external contracts; and Margaret Beck and Gillian Gilks, the greatest doubles pair in the world, said they would never play together again.

9 Break with Beck

Gillian and Maggie Beck had been doubles partners for seven years. Not exclusively, but with very great frequency, particularly at the highest level. Ever since they overtook the other brilliant pairing of Margaret Boxall and Sue Whetnall, they had won more open tournaments than any other pair in Britain, and internationally were, though not unbeatable, at least less likely to be beaten than any other combination from any nation. They were the reigning European, Commonwealth and world invitation champions and had only just lost their All-England title, and that does not leave a lot to be said. But as we have seen, they differed from Boxall and Whetnall in one supremely important fact: they were constantly fighting each other in singles finals in the same tournaments in which, an hour later, they had to combine in the closest harmony. Possibly no other partnership in racket sports has had to survive — or has survived — that pressure. In badminton, Kobbero and Hammergaard Hansen, Tjun Tjun and Wahjudi, the Devlin sisters, Boxall and Whetnall, were all fine singles players, but never were any of them at any time the two best singles players in the world. (It is the same in tennis. There have been great doubles teams of outstanding singles rivals, though apart from Newcombe and Roche they don't come easily to mind, but greatest teams of all have been those who almost certainly would not carry equal expectation of singles success, such as Hewitt and McMillan, and Casals and King.) And then there came Beck and Gilks, and it was probably inevitable that the BAE should, at an early stage, have put together these two outstanding youngsters, clearly destined for tremendous success. Even with hindsight, it would not be fair to criticise the Association for not foreseeing the problem — seven years of doubles success, for heaven's sake, is a good enough answer to that. In the end, one day, the break was bound to come, and Gillian confirms all that one had feared.

'We were both too interested in singles, that was the trouble, and gradually the pressure of continually fighting each other on the singles court took its toll. It was forever happening: we'd meet in the singles final and one of us had to lose. Then we'd go on court together for the doubles final, and there were problems. For Maggie, singles had always been the main game — she came comparatively late to doubles at international level, and hardly ever played mixed — and I think it's fair to say that if I'd beaten her in the singles, she would be angry right through the doubles. But we were quite good friends for a long while, and played together until we weren't.

'The parting would have been all right, but for the most unfortunate way in which it happened. I had decided that year that I just couldn't play with Maggie any more, but I was reluctant to tell her so. That summer Margaret Boxall was getting married and moving away, so I asked Sue Whetnall whether she would like to team up with me. Naturally, before she could give me an answer, she asked Margaret Boxall to confirm that she wasn't going to be available to play with her. She wasn't, and that was fine. That left me free to talk to Maggie. The trouble was that Margaret talked to her before I did, telling her how surprised she was that Maggie and I were splitting up. And that was the first Maggie knew of it. It was desperately unfortunate, and I would never have wanted it to be like that, but almost no one was to blame. I suppose I should have started by talking to Maggie Beck about it, but I didn't want to upset her unnecessarily.

'Anyway, that's the way it happened. I played with Sue, and Maggie teamed up with Nora Gardner, which was fair enough. They were a very good pair. But the ill-feeling the incident caused triggered off the waves of bitterness and resentment that have been coming my way from the BAE ever since. It didn't help that, as we all knew, Maggie Beck was about to marry Ron Lockwood, the chairman of selectors and the man who captained most of our teams.'

However unhappy was the prelude to the season, the fact was that Gillian Gilks immediately returned to the singles supremacy that she had not fully experienced since the rise of Maggie Beck. For a long time it seemed nobody in the world was going to stop her (she won the first five of her encounters with Miss Beck and only lost to her once in the whole season), and as the playing months went by, Gillian rose to a badminton climax the majesty of which was unequalled. In the first four weeks of the season, between Sunday October 5th and Saturday November 1st, 1975, she won the English invitation singles, the Surrey Restricted, the Worcestershire, Lincolnshire and Wimbledon Open singles, all without losing a game. On three of the four possible occasions she was triple champion. On the fourth, the Worcestershire, her failure to win was not because of any loss of points: Elliot Stuart, her partner, walked out before the final because, he said, he had to wait more than seven hours after winning his semi.

Mrs Gilks was furious, and the BAE were not too happy either. Regarding the matter as a major scandal, they suspended the All-England mixed champion *sine die*, pending their next council meeting — having taken into account what the Emergency Committee called his 'generally unsatisfactory conduct' in tournaments the previous season. The recommendation was for a suspension of two months from October 22nd, which put Stuart out of the first two Thomas Cup matches, against Scotland and Holland, but meant that he was available for the crucial third round against Denmark. Stuart, who had then been capped for England 26 times and was the first international ever to be suspended by the Association, said at the time that he would not play against Denmark either, whatever the decision of the council. He later relented, but in the event was not picked anyway.

The English Invitation singles did not proceed quite as expected. Beck and Gilks won their pools with ludicrous ease as usual (even Jane Webster, an international and the former junior champion, only managed four points against Gillian), but Heather Nielsen conceded her pool by losing a tight match against the current junior champion, Paula Kilvington, and poor Sue Whetnall damaged leg ligaments in the very first game she played. This let under-15 champion Karen Bridge through to the semi-finals, where she extended Maggie Beck to 11–4, 12–9. Three weeks later, the Lincolnshire — not a top tournament attraction, but included that season on the Hearts of Oak circuit, the winning of which was a fairly important matter. Gillian's two doubles finals were worth remembering: in the women's, Sue Whetnall's leg had recovered sufficiently for them to meet and beat the Maggie Beck-Nora Gardner partnership, and in the mixed (for which Derek Talbot came in for Stuart), they beat in the final by only 18–17, 17–14 the new team of Mike Tredgett and Nora Gardner, later to become the most brilliant mixed pair in the world.

In the four weeks from the middle of November Gillian played in another four major tournaments, remained undefeated in singles play and lost only one match — a doubles at the Northumberland Open, in which she was playing with Barbara Giles. This was the territory of Margaret Boxall's husband, Eddie Allen, and the Boxall-Whetnall team were together again. Giles and Gilks went down in the final to Beck and Gardner, 15–13 in the third. The last of those four tournaments was the English National championships, in which Gillian made history by becoming the first player of either sex to win all three titles. Playing the last match against Maggie before she became Mrs Lockwood, Gillian won 11–0, 11–7; she and Sue Whetnall beat Beck and Gardner 11–5, 11–5, and she and Derek Talbot beat Tredgett and Gardner 15–10, 15–12. This last was a magnificent match, the result of which meant that Gillian had won the mixed for eight of the past nine years, with three different partners.

There were another seven open tournaments in the first eight weeks of the New Year with triple victories in four of them. Three of the singles wins were overseas, the Swedish, Dutch and German Opens, and in the final of each she beat the Danish star, Lene Koppen. One doubles she and Mrs Whetnall lost to Nora Gardner and Maggie Lockwood, their only defeat; and once she and Derek Talbot lost a mixed, in Germany to Skovgaard and Koppen. It was a staggering accumulation of triumph, marred by the loss of only one singles match: on January 22nd, Mrs Lockwood beat her in the Hearts of Oak circuit final, 8–11, 11–2, 11–8 — her first loss to the former Miss Beck since November 1974, and her only one until November 1976.

In the middle of this bag of badminton jewels in the 1975–6 season, another stone came Gillian's way, glittering and totally unexpected. On November 29th a letter arrived at Swerford Villa, Steyning, in a long, white envelope. It was marked as boldly as anything 'On Her Majesty's Service' and there were other, less ostentatious printings on it. One said 'Urgent', one said 'Personal' and in the bottom left-hand corner were the words 'Prime Minister'. Well if you ever get a letter like that towards the end of the year, it may be that this is what it will say:

'From the Principal Private Secretary: 10 Downing Street.

Madam,

The Prime Minister has asked me to inform you, in strict confidence, that he has it in mind, on the occasion of the forthcoming list of New Year Honours, to submit your name to The Queen with a recommendation that Her Majesty may be graciously pleased to approve that you be appointed a Member of the Order of the British Empire.

Before doing so, the Prime Minister would be glad to be assured that this would be agreeable to you. I should be grateful if you would let me know by completing the enclosed form and sending it to me by return of post.

I am, Madam,

Your obedient Servant'

On January 2nd the Press spill the beans and from that day on the phone calls and the telegrams and the letters sweep in. Everybody is so vastly pleased for you, and say all the nice things they have wanted to say for years and forget, for a day or two at least, anything remotely nasty. Amid Gillian's great pile of congratulations two seem to the outsider to be particularly memorable. One contained the sentence: 'If all players had such good court manners as you, we umpires would have an easier task.' The other, from a senior male player whose privacy must be respected, read as follows:

'How wonderful to read your name in the New Year's Honours List. To have achieved so much at such a young age is a record that, in another sphere, would have made yours a household name. My wife and I are proud to know you. As far as your natural modesty allows, try to ensure that the BA of E makes some capital out of your success, for the sake of future generations of players.'

A few days later comes a dull, brown envelope addressed to Mrs Gillian M. Gilks, MBE, from the Central Chancery of the Orders of Knighthood, St James's Palace, and this gives you your marching orders:

'Madam,

I am commanded to inform you that an Investiture will be held at Buckingham Palace on Tuesday, 24th February, 1976, at which your attendance is requested.

I am desired to say that you should arrive at the Palace between the hours of 10 o'clock and 10.30 a.m. and this letter should be shown on entering the gates of the Palace, as no other card of admission is issued to recipients. Cars may be parked in the inner Quadrangle of the Palace under police direction. No windscreen tickets are issued.

If desired, two guests are permitted to accompany you to watch the Ceremony, and tickets for them may be obtained by making application on the form enclosed herewith which should be returned to me as soon as possible.

The only exception to this rule is that, if a recipient wishes to bring with her her husband and two sons, or two daughters, or a son and daughter, a third ticket will be issued, but in NO circumstances will a fourth ticket be issued.

DRESS

(a) Serving Officers and Other Ranks of the Women's Royal Naval Service, Women's Royal Army Corps, Women's Royal Air Force and Members of the Police Force and Fire Brigades should wear the dress laid down in the regulations of their respective Service. Orders, Decorations and Medals should not be worn.

(b) Civilians may, if they so desire, wear the uniform of the Civil Organization or Service to which they belong; otherwise they should wear Day Dress. Orders, Decorations and Medals should not be worn.

I am, Madam,

Your obedient servant

The Prime Minister's Principal Private Secretary, you will note, was an obedient Servant. This Major-General was just an obedient servant. They are obviously accustomed to trouble about tickets for sons and daughters and so on, because the whole of that sentence was thickly underlined in red.

Being unsure, as many of us might be, as to just what constitutes day dress, or even Day Dress, Gillian telephoned for advice and chose a black floral print dress, with lace trimming. On the phone they told her about gloves, which must be either both on or both carried, but NEVER one of each. What they didn't mention was hats. 'It never occurred to me,' said Gillian, who probably hadn't worn a hat since the day she was married, 'that I was supposed to wear one indoors. I was horrified to find that I was almost the only woman there without one.' In the good old days, apparently, they would have turned her away for such a misdemeanour, but standards aren't what they used to be and she wasn't even fined. Investitures, which go on throughout much of the year, are not always held by the Queen, but this was one of her days on, to Gillian's delight. It is, as you can imagine, a conveyor belt job. The recipients are swiftly separated from their guests (Gillian took her husband and her mother) and shuffled off to queue in alphabetical order in an anteroom devoted to their particular Order.

'You don't see much of the proceedings, you're just edging forward in this queue getting nearer the entrance all the time. You come in across one end of the room, and they tell you just what to do: it's so many steps forward, so many paces towards the Queen, a curtsey in somewhere and so many paces backwards before you turn and go off again. We were warned that she doesn't shake hands, she just holds it out and you touch it — if she shook with everybody she'd have no hand left. She doesn't say much either. I mean, there's no time, is there? She's getting through hundreds in a couple of hours. I did meet her before, less formally, at the Commonwealth Games in Christchurch, when there was a vast garden party for the team and she and Princess Anne and Mark Phillips were there and came round and chatted. I thought then how pretty she was, but like a fragile paper doll, with her face powdered over.'

Afterwards, the photographs, and the Palace are very firm about when and where. Family cameras may be used in the inner Quadrangle, but may not be taken into the Palace; other personal photographers will not be admitted, and such pictures must be taken outside the forecourt gates. A number of Press photographers and film cameramen have permission to operate in the Quadrangle as recipients leave the investiture, and a commercial firm are happily rooted out there banging off colour photographs as hard as they can go. Anyway, it was all a tremendous honour for badminton as well as for Gillian, and a day of great pleasure and excitement.

Soon afterwards, she was back in the business of building her strength and fitness for the All-England, an exhausting procedure to which she had been applying herself all the season under the guidance of her new coach, Michael Goodwin. Three days a week she travelled up from Steyning to a health farm near High Barnet where John Conteh used to train (more of the ghastly details later), and as a result reckoned that, whatever her badminton was like, she was going to be the fittest woman in the world by the time the championships began. Certainly her first two opponents were in no mood to argue against the idea, winning as they did only nine points between them. A bit of a ding-dong with Joke van Beusekom and an extraordinary 11–0, 12–10 win over Lene Koppen, and Gillian was in the final for the fourth consecutive year.

Even before advancing so far, she was a warm favourite for the title. No European was likely to beat her on current form, Tati Sumirah was the only Indonesian with half a chance, and the Japanese (who had won the women's singles title five times in the preceding seven years) were this year exercising a boycott on the All-England. This unlikely state of affairs deserves some political explanation. For several years the Peoples' Republic of China (mainland China, or 'Red' China, as some liked to call it) had been applying for admission to the IBF. They would almost certainly have been successful but for the fact that their application was always accompanied by the condition that Taiwan should be expelled. The same situation had occurred in other sports, and in some was still occurring. Some gave way to the demand, some did not. The perfectly reasonable attitude of the IBF was that, as long as Taiwan paid their dues and behaved themselves, there was no way in which they could honourably be expelled from the Federation; and that the IBF had no particular objection to two Chinese bodies being affiliated, since it was clear that neither one could adequately represent the interests of players belonging to the other.

The PRC, however, would have none of that sweet reason. To them, Taiwan was but a province, albeit an offshore one, and it had no right at all to individual membership of anything. At the annual meeting of the Federation in the summer of 1975, a motion by Sweden called for the resignation from the IBF of Taiwan. It was supported by 49 votes to 25, but as such a motion could only be passed with a three-quarters majority, it failed. The voting system at the IBF meetings is based on a scale of from one to three votes per nation, according to the number of affiliated players and their participation in the Thomas and Uber Cups. Proposals by Pakistan, Thailand and Czechoslovakia to alter this to one vote per member nation irrespective of its size needed a two-thirds majority to succeed, and narrowly failed to achieve it, 46 votes to 27.

At the IBF Council meeting the next day, the Asian Badminton Confederation handed a letter to the President protesting at the 'unreasonable attitude of a handful of representatives and the iniquitous system of voting rights presently existing.' Clearly feeling that the BAE was at the bottom of this, in collusion with the other three British associations, the Asians announced that they were going to direct their member nations not to allow any of their players to take part in the All-England championships. In fact, an entirely new tournament, the Asian Invitation, was organised in Bangkok to coincide with the All-England, depriving the Wembley championships of many of the players it was looking forward to welcoming. The Indonesians split their strength between the two: both Hartono and Liem Swie King were at Wembley, but Miss Verawaty was in Bangkok; and though Tjun Tjun and Wahjudi were defending their All-England title, Chandra and Christian were not challenging them. The Japanese boycotted the London meeting entirely, which removed the strongest overseas contender from the women's battlefield — but Hiroe Yuki did not appear in Bangkok either.

So, without too much agony, Gillian Gilks was in the final again. Great things were happening in the other half of the draw too. Having come quietly through the first two rounds, Maggie Lockwood struggled over Annette Borjesson, of Sweden; then she destroyed Wendy Clarkson (Canada) 11–1, 11–1 in the quarter-final and in the semi overwhelmed the second seed, Tati Sumirah, by 11–1, 11–0 in 12 minutes. It was a performance of such authority, despite some trouble with an ankle for which she had been having pain-killing injections, that Mrs Gilks must have seen the spectre of 1973 rising all over again.

In the other female sections Britons were beaming too. Nora Gardner and Mrs Lockwood won a tremendous semi-final battle with Indonesia's Masli and Widiastuti, and faced Gillian and Sue Whetnall in the doubles final; and Miss Gardner reached the mixed final again, to defend the title she had won in 1975 with Elliot Stuart. This time she was playing with Mike Tredgett against Gillian and Derek Talbot. British men had not fared too well otherwise, but Rudy Hartono had won a 65-minute match with Flemming Delfs (18–15 in the third) and was going for his record eighth singles crown. As his opponent was his young compatriot Liem Swie King, few badminton players had any doubt about the result of the match.

It was not long before there was no doubt about the result of the women's singles, either. Mrs Gilks was all quicksilver, wrote John Ballantine in *The Sunday Times*: 'at once gracefully feline, yet deadly as a striking shrike. She hit delicate touch shots that grazed the net and then back-pedalled on her toes like a ballerina to hammer smashes on to the lines.' The first game lasted only five-and-a-half minutes, 11–0. The second took twice as long, 11–3, but poor Maggie was never in the game. Judy Hashman,

The greatest of all triumphs: in 1976, Gillian was triple champion of the All-England. She beat Maggie Lockwood (formerly Beck) in the singles final and with Sue Whetnall (below) *beat Lockwood and Nora Gardner to win the doubles*

More joy on the great day: Gillian and Derek Talbot beating Mike Tredgett and Nora Gardner in the 1976 mixed final. And somewhere in the middle of the Wembley hubbub, Mike Gilks snatches a kiss with the wife from whom he is soon to part

reporting the final for *Badminton Gazette*, wrote that she 'gave a lack-lustre and dispirited performance which did no credit to herself or the game and had no place on finals day at Wembley ... Her three points were more than she deserved.' That gives too little credit to Gillian Gilks, who for once had come on to court for an All-England final looking and feeling as though her opponent had not a chance in hell of winning. From the first stroke, she imposed her game on the woman on the other side of the net. On the occasions when Gillian was able to do that, nobody could live with her. Hiroe Yuki or no, we were looking that afternoon at unbeatable badminton. When she went on to win the other two titles as well, each one in two games, Gillian climbed the game's highest mountain. No woman had won the triple crown at the All-England championships since Tonny Ahm, of Denmark, in 1952 — and in those days it was very much a European affair. No English woman had done it since Kitty McKane, more than half a century before Gillian.

Observers at the scene were as much astonished by what went on before the match as by the play itself. She was on the practice court for an hour immediately before the final 'to exhaust my nervous condition and get really relaxed.' She followed the stroke play session with 10 strenuous minutes of exercises, at the end of which she was as supple as a spoonful of mercury. Mrs Hashman, reported in the national Press as saying 'I would never have done that in my day,' was anxious to qualify that in the *Gazette* by pointing out that when she was champion she was either a student or held a full-time job, and that anyway it was not necessary to her game 'to such an enlarged extent.' She then went on to analyse, with a suspicion of sourness, Gillian's preparation:

'All champions have their weaknesses, be they destructive nerves, slowness of foot, problems with sight and recognition, problems of a mental or intellectual nature, or with stroke production. The range is large, the combinations many. To accept your weaknesses is the greatest problem. Then you have to work on them. Gillian has at last accepted hers, which to my mind were three of the above. She has now done something about them, which is what other champions before her have done but without the attendant publicity. All champions have their own form of dedication. Many things are given up or delayed, such as the financial, social, career and family sides of life. Her weaknesses required a fantastic, fanatical programme to overcome them, because they were of that nature. To imply that such a programme is necessary for all future champions is wrong. That she believed so completely in the programme that it became the basis for her win, and that she completed it so thoroughly, says much for the girl.'

10 Superwoman

If you accept Judy Hashman's analysis of the potential weaknesses of champions — and nobody is more likely to be right than she is — and her belief that Gillian Gilks suffered from three of them, you will probably come to the conclusion that the new All-England queen's danger areas were slowness of foot, destructive nerves and 'problems of a mental or intellectual nature.' I doubt if the new champion herself would have argued much about the assessment. She has often said that, however hard she worked at her physical training, her mobility on the court suffered badly in comparison with that of Margaret Beck, just as the tall Flemming Delf's does against that of Liem Swie King. They can reach much further in all directions, but it takes longer to get their feet to the right spot.

Nerves? Nobody who watched Gillian at the All-England through the 1970s needs reminding that she often started her matches like a ghost in torment, unable to produce even competent badminton. We were not to know that, confronted by a critical singles match, the lady has often been so in the grip of her own nervous system that she has been physically sick before entering the arena, like many an actress on a first night in the theatre. And mental problems? That does not imply that Gillian Gilks was a dum-dum (her 'A' levels abolish that thought), but that psychologically she was not well equipped to win hard matches. 'I wanted to win all right,' she said. 'The trouble was that when I went on court my predominant feeling was "I don't want to lose".' Somehow, by the end of March 1976, Gillian had been if not transformed, at least immeasurably strengthened. She became as different a player by those championships as she was as 'different' a person in the autumn of 1980 when she appeared with a new nose and a new hairstyle.

You could see it coming right through the season, the statistics of which are quite ridiculous. In seventeen open tournaments plus the English invitation singles and the Hearts of Oak circuit finals, she won ten triple titles and six double (the odd one out being the invitation singles). In those tournaments, she lost only one singles match, two doubles and two mixed. If you extend the season beyond the domestic one and include the immediately-following European, Guernsey and United States championships, as well as delving into seven county meetings in which she was involved, you find that between October 4th, 1975 and May 1st, 1976 (30 weeks),

Gillian played a total of 259 badminton matches and lost only 13 of them, five of which were doubles matches in team contests. Even given her extraordinary talent and dedication, something must have remarkably affected Mrs Gilks before and during this season, at the absolute end of which she was triple champion of Europe, the Commonwealth and the world (which is what the All-England victories were accepted as meaning). The catalyst, without any doubt, was her coach, Michael Goodwin.

You would find a lot of takers for the theory that the union of Gilks and Goodwin has been an unfortunate one for badminton. The Badminton Association of England would probably be the first through the door to sign the proposition, because from that determined and obstinate partnership came more trouble for the establishment than it had known in the previous 80 years of its existence. We don't all support the BAE's 'black sheep' syndrome, and perhaps the principles of the matter could be discussed later. Here the concern is a matter of practicality, a matter of coaching.

All her badminton life Gillian has been used to having a coach. Even at the age of nine, in the Cheam club, Eric Kinsman came along once a fortnight to advise on the basics of the game. A year or so later, she was picked up by one of the most successful talent-spotters of the country, Ian Palmer, and joined his group of highly-promising children at Wimbledon. When she hit international level, at the age of 16, she passed into the care of the national coach, Jake Downey. He remained the major influence on her game until she felt the need for a closer, more personal adviser, and that was Mike Goodwin. Each man, she says firmly, was superb in his own field. Goodwin was exactly what she needed at the time: 'There's no doubt I wouldn't have won the All-England without him. He made the difference between being a runner-up and a winner.'

Downey was a high-level, deep-thinking coach; a philosopher whose theory was that the game of badminton is a battle. Goodwin took it on from there, providing the finishing touches that Gillian was not able to produce alone. He gave her kick, determined aggression: 'I don't have a very aggressive attitude in everyday life, unless I am provoked. If you are provoked on court, you might lose your temper, and that is the wrong sort of aggression. It has to be controlled, and somehow Mike instilled that in me.'

An extremely placid person, Gillian acutely needed the mental attitude towards which Goodwin directed her. But in purely practical terms, even at the age of 25 and at the cultured and sophisticated stage which her stroke play had reached, Goodwin was able to lead her to strokes she hadn't tried before. At the net, for instance, where she spent so much of her doubles life, she learned not just to spin the shuttle, but to tumble and spin at the same time, a shot the opponent finds it very difficult to judge accurately.

'If you slice across the base of the shuttle, it causes it to spin in the air, but it proceeds in a fairly straightforward, smooth action, and an experienced opponent can judge the way it is spinning and counteract it. If you can turn it at the same time that you are spinning it, there is no way the opponent can judge which way it's going to come off his racket. Thanks to Mike, I added that to my repertoire. Then there's a particular overhead stroke that we call a reverse slice: instead of being a straightforward forehand slice it's played on a round-the-head stroke, a round-the-head forehand instead of a backhand. Instead of just stroking it down, you actually hit fast across the shuttle, and this causes it to spin and to die very quickly.'

No quality is more important in badminton than deception. Because the deceleration of the shuttle is so pronounced, the most devastating smash can be returned if the opponent happens to be correctly positioned. Power of shot alone never won a match, though it often does in tennis. But because the muscle power does not have to be prodigious, the possibilities for masked deflection are the greater; and, most devastating of all, the unreadable drop smash can be exercised — the overhead blow in which, at the last instant, the flashing racket head is held back so that it caresses the shuttle instead of punishing it.

Goodwin's first move was to harden Gillian's game, to give it more speed and more attack, which coincided naturally with strengthening her resolve and increasing her mental aggression. Later he turned the emphasis towards deception, towards a game that her opponents would find it more difficult to read. There was time for that later. First he had to put fire in her belly (and keep it there, which wasn't easy at 26 years, when everything had been won) and he was determined to do something for her that had never happened in badminton before: to make her fit. Not just fit enough, but super-fit, the fittest woman in the world, as he put it — or, more realistically, the fittest woman in Britain. In practice, the challenge was handed to a man named Eddie Chapman, who ran a health farm at Shenley Lodge, near Potters Bar. Most of his time was spent in reducing the girths of the Rolls-Royce set, but Chapman knew a bit about bringing sportsmen to a peak, too — it was at Shenley that John Conteh received his finishing touches before he won the world light-heavyweight title.

Now, the rest of us, hard pressed to make the third flight of stairs, would have said that Gillian Gilks was fit enough already, certainly fit enough for badminton. Never a day went by without her running and skipping and shuttle-running and so on, and what more do you want? Chapman wanted a lot more. For an international sportswoman, particularly one who was training to become a world champion, he thought her standard of fitness was deplorable. The initial tests designed to discover her weaknesses disclosed enough to fill a book: solar plexus, shoulders, chest — even her arms, for a racket sport, were nothing like strong enough. And he made some very rude remarks about her agility. The cure was simple, but not without pain. Three or four days a week for four months, she was to leave her home at Steyning at 8.0 a.m. and make the two-hour journey to Shenley Lodge. There she would train for two hours, and later play badminton for two hours before the two-hour car-train-car journey brought her home at 8.0 p.m. A hell of a way to pass the day. Remembering that the weekends were almost exclusively taken up with

Gillian Gilks — a smasher

Mike Goodwin, the coach who turned Gillian from a runner-up to a winner, gets to work at the courtside

tournament play, it may not be irrelevant to point out that by the following summer the Gilks marriage was over.

Chapman trained her as if she were a professional fighter, using highly-sophisticated muscle-building equipment. Her 90-minute morning workout brought guilt and shame in successive waves to the non-athletic spectator, shortly followed by the seizure of his joints in aching rigidity. Circles, weights, bars, pulleys, arms, legs, twists, turns, bends and torture — nothing was exempt from Chapman's examination. Even shadow boxing and ballet kicking were used to extend her agility and improve her reactions. There was one appalling test of arm stamina that involved rolling a weighted bar up ropes, which she could only do three times when she started. The average man manages 10 repetitions, John Conteh did 60 and Gillian got to 40 by the end. It is mind over matter, that's all, she says. Your arms ache terribly, but you must beat the ache with your head. You are supposed to do the exercise with your arms straight out in front of you. When Paula Kilvington began training with Goodwin she soon discovered it was much easier to roll the bar with the arms bent. Goodwin soon discovered the cure for that: a cigarette lighter held under the elbows — alight!

People who have never played badminton, and particularly those who don't even watch it, seem to have the idea it is a cissy game. A training schedule like that ought to dispel the suggestion. One hour of badminton, the experts say, can be at least as exhausting as three hours of tennis. Tennis demands greater stamina and endurance, but badminton is more explosive and the player must be capable of producing the explosions even in the last minutes of a match. To do that, everything in your body has to be in perfect condition, from top to bottom. Muscles must be strong, but if they are too heavy they will slow the player down, detract from her explosive qualities. Just the same, chunky players like Indonesia's doubles wizard Ade Chandra, and Saori Kondo of Japan, who twice reached the All-England singles final, seem to get by pretty well. You might think that you could spot the ideal badminton physique, but practice does not confirm any theories in the matter. When you see among the world's outstanding players bodies of such disparity as those of Kondo and Mrs Gilks, Liem Swie King and Flemming Delfs, Nora Perry and Lene Koppen, you realise there is no such thing as the perfect badminton body.

Whatever shape and weight it is, it has to remain as light as a feather even when it feels as heavy as lead, and that's what Eddie Chapman's agony chamber was trying to do for Gillian. Every morning the gym work was followed by a two-mile run, before the relief of ultra-sonic and ultra-violet treatment, massage and a light lunch. Eating during a tournament, particularly on finals day, can be a problem. With an important singles match to face, Gillian has to eat about four hours beforehand, because it takes that long to digest the food. Steak or fried food are out, because they are not easily digestible, and salad alone does not provide sufficient energy. Gillian goes for something like breast of chicken and plenty of good vegetables, though you do meet players who put their faith in brown bread and honey and a bar of chocolate. Because of the comparatively short time for which you are likely to be on court, drinking doesn't present the problem that it does in tennis. Gillian often drinks between games — water, lemon barley or perhaps a glucose-based energising fluid.

Whatever habits of nourishment and preparation the player has, they will have been designed to stave off the awful moment when the body cries out 'I'm tired'. By then breathing will have got so difficult that the whole chest is tight and it hurts just to lift your arms. When that hits you, you hope you're serving, so you can walk slowly to the shuttle and take time to pick it up. Every second's respite is a blessing then. If your opponent is serving and can see you're in that sort of trouble, she will get back quickly and get on with the game. In a long hard match, both parties are likely to indulge in some time-wasting: tieing a shoe-lace, towelling your hands or your face, wiping your glasses — one player almost on his knees with exhaustion had the brilliant idea of pretending a contact lens had fallen out, and took a full minute on the floor to find it. Play must, of course, be continuous and umpires do their best not to let players get away with too much, but, hang it all, a chap can't play when he can't see, can he?

A long badminton rally will almost certainly leave both players in some kind of oxygen debt, and the one who can replace the deficiency soonest is the one who is going to see the match out in the best condition. By the time Gillian Gilks reached the 1976 All-England, she had got to the state where neither her body nor her mind would admit tiredness on a badminton court. Two deep breaths and she was back on top, knowing that she had the beating of the woman on the other side of the net. Chapman rated her there at least 25 per cent fitter than anybody else on court. 'She made some of her opponents look like cart-horses and I doubt if there's a woman in the world who could compare to her now,' he said at the time. A basis of such extraordinary fitness brought its own psychological advantages and was a perfect foundation on which Goodwin could build the confidence of a natural conqueror, the aggression that develops from absolute determination. In short, Gillian needed a damned good push and that's just what she got.

Enthusiasm, drive, advice — if a player is offered and can accept all three from her coach, the relationship is probably a good one, though no player is likely to agree entirely with the advice offered or the methods used. The admirable Jake Downey was, in the end, too theoretical a coach to get the best out of Gillian, a trend underlined by the fact that they lived far apart and had no specific meeting place, so that she was more or less following a correspondence course on the game. Mike Goodwin, apart from being able to strike exactly the right chord for Gillian as a motivator, was an admirable analyst of her game and that of her potential opponent. 'If I haven't been able to watch the girl play, Mike will make certain he has. He'll tell me the strokes she's got and where he thinks she is weak. His ability to analyse anything makes him a better coach than most — he can sit up all night working things out. He'll talk a problem over from every single point of view, not just his own. He shows me all the pitfalls and makes me weigh up which way it should go, and if at the end of it all I don't know what to do, we'll do it his way.'

After a match a coach is invaluable, because he will have watched it in a way that nobody else could. Even an experienced player is not going to be able to answer the questions that one of the participants will want to put. To the spectator it was another game, another contest; to the coach concerned, it was an examination, an exercise, and his absence from the courtside can be a considerable handicap to a struggling player. The rise of the remarkable Indonesian woman, Wiharjo Verawaty, provided an interesting example of this. She had not looked like a threat to Mrs Gilks of any great significance until the Randers tournament in Denmark in November 1979, when she burst through to beat Lene Koppen in the semi and Gillian in the final, in each case without losing a game. 'Everything she did was spot on. She beat me with strength, power and speed, and I didn't know what to do about it. All I knew was that she was a lot stronger than me. When you're playing against someone as tall and strong as that, you sometimes can't even tell if you are hitting a good length. Normally, a girl can only hit hard from three-quarters of the way back, but Verawaty can put a smash away from the back line. Mike wasn't over there, and if he had been he couldn't have helped me during the match; but he would have analysed her play against Lene, and after my match he would have been able to tell me just what went wrong and how I should try to tackle her next time.'

Verawaty went on to become in March 1980 the first Indonesian woman to reach the All-England singles final (beating the two Japanese stars, Yonekura and Hiroe Yuki, on the way) and a few weeks later she won the world championship. But this was March 1976, and superfit Gillian Gilks was the queen. Superfit was the way she had to stay, because in the next four weeks she would be playing in Dublin, Philadelphia and Guernsey, and a month later she would be in Indonesia.

II Double trouble

It was immediately before her triumph at the 1976 All-England that Gillian Gilks had her first serious brush with the badminton authority. Predictably, it was over what she had long thought of as one of those hateful internationals that had become a tradition in the game, when the leading English players were required to turn out in some distant corner of the land a few days before the All-England began. Often the matches had been on the Monday night of the tournament week. In 1976, the match was against Indonesia at Washington, County Durham, on the Thursday of the previous week — an encounter notable, incidentally, for the fact that it was the first time the two nations had met in England, and the first time the men had ever met. Mrs Gilks faced her two doubles (partnering Sue Whetnall and Derek Talbot) with her usual reluctance, for she had come to regard these fixtures as seriously impinging on her preparation schedule for the year's most important tournament.

Ten days earlier, Margaret Lockwood, who was due to play the singles against Indonesia, had injured her leg in Germany, and because of the uncertainty of her full recovery, Gillian was asked to stand by to take her place. This pleased Gillian even less and when it got to an hour before the match and no decision had been taken about Mrs Lockwood, Gillian told Ron Lockwood (the team captain) that she was not at all keen to play the singles. In the end, Maggie played (and easily beat Taty Sumirah), but harsh words passed between Ron Lockwood and Gillian over her reluctance to deputise for his wife. The incident undoubtedly was recorded in the minds of some of the BAE officials as a black mark against Mrs Gilks. Within a year there were to be many more.

Meanwhile, this incredible season of 1975–6 pursued its golden path — though not without a stumble. A week after the All-England, the team went to Dublin for the European championships and on the second day lost the title they had held for the previous two years. After beating Sweden 4–1 and West Germany 3–2 (with Gillian conceding only eight points in her two singles matches), England faced Denmark in what was to be the deciding encounter of the tournament. The decision could not have been finer. With Gillian surprisingly losing her singles to Lene Koppen 11–4, 12–10 (Miss Koppen was 6–0 up in the second), and losing the mixed with Talbot to Koppen and Steen Skovgaard, England lost the tie by 3–2. That meant both England and Denmark had won two ties and lost one; both had won nine individual matches; but England had won 21 games to the 20 of Denmark, and it was publicly announced that England had retained the championship. Congratulations all round, but not from the Danes. They immediately lodged a protest and the calculators came out again. True enough, England had won 21 games, but they had lost 15 while Denmark had lost only 14, so the game differences were the same. Rightly enough, the championship was decided by the result between the two sides.

A disappointing start, but the individual championships were immediately under way. Paul Whetnall was England's main hope in the men's singles, and he reached the semi-finals before going out to the eventual champion, Flemming Delfs — rather surprisingly referred to in *The Daily Telegraph* as 'the Danish youth'. Our two men's pairs reached their final quite magnificently, by beating the two top-seeded pairs in the semis, and Stevens and Tredgett took the title with an enthralling win, 13–15, 15–12, 15–6, over Talbot and Eddie Sutton. The English women's pairs of Lockwood and Gardner, Gilks and Whetnall, also met in the final (15–8, 15–4 to Gilks and Whetnall). The less said about that the better, reported the *Badminton Gazette*, because it produced some deplorable badminton with hardly a decent rally throughout. In the mixed Talbot and Gilks found themselves facing for the gold medal the Danish pair who had beaten them to win the team title — Skovgaard and Koppen. Revenge came in the tightest possible finish of a brilliant match: 6–15, 15–12, 17–15. 'We didn't deserve to win,' recalled Gillian. 'We set at 14–14 in the third, and Steen threw away match point through sheer nerves. He had an absolute sitter to smash, took it halfway down his racket and hit into the net.' But win they did, and that completed a dream for Gillian Gilks. She was triple champion of All-England, the Commonwealth and Europe.

Three of England's four representatives in the women's singles had reached the semis — the surprise being Sue Whetnall's two-game defeat of the seeded Lonny Bostofte. Both Gillian and Maggie Lockwood had stormed through the early rounds without losing a game — Mrs Lockwood including a devastating win, 11–1, 11–1, over the former All-England and European champion, Eva Stuart — but there was, of course, Lene Koppen fizzing away at the bottom end of the draw. If there was any doubt that she was in top form, it was dispelled in the quarter-finals, when she destroyed her neighbouring seed, Eva Kranz, 11–0, 11–0. Both Lene and Gillian reached the final with two-game wins, and faced each other for the title as they had done in Vienna two years earlier. Mrs Gilks had shaken off the effects of the cold she was suffering during the team championships, and had her finger on the winning button from the first stroke. With Koppen serving poorly, and apparently distracted by a crying baby in the gallery, Gilks raced away to an 8–0 lead and took the game 11–6. The standard of play was much higher in the second game. It produced several splendid rallies, and the scores were level at 6–6 and 10–10, but the champion's superior net play took her through the match in only 22 minutes.

Straight from Dublin Gillian went for the first time to the United States, to compete in their Open that started the next day. With her from the Europeans went an interesting handful of players, all invited with travel and accommodation paid: Joke van Beusekom, Lene Koppen, Sue Whetnall, David Eddy, Ray Stevens, Paul Whetnall, Kihlstrom and Froman of Sweden, and Braun and Maywald of West Germany. Despite jet lag and the appallingly humid heat of Philadelphia, there was again virtually no opposition for Gilks and Koppen until they met in the final. In a temperature of 92 degrees Fahrenheit they played for 39 minutes, with 69 changes of service. Gillian ran out to win the third game with six consecutive winning points in one hand. With Paul Whetnall winning the men's singles, every title went to the visiting Europeans. It is probably true to say that no truly amateur sport flourishes in the USA. The colleges and universities concentrate on those activities that can lead to a living for the participants. Other sports have to fight for themselves, often without financial or administrative backing; and beyond the educational circle, the vast size of the country makes it extraordinarily difficult to organise amateur sport on a national basis. That is why there has been perhaps only one American player since Judy Hashman to become well-known to the badminton public, and that was Tyna Barinaga.

The sort of problems that confront American badminton were certainly unknown at Gillian's next port of call: St Peter Port, Guernsey. In this enthusiastic little island, everyone who wields a racket knows everyone who owns a shuttlecock. In this Spring of 1976 they were celebrating the golden jubilee of their Association (and, more privately, the greatest success ever achieved by a member, the winning by Sally Leadbeater of the All-England Under-15 singles title) and invited a handful of English players to stiffen the standard of their annual open tournament. The results were predictable and not important, except that the women's doubles was won by Gillian Gilks and Anne Statt, a lady who was soon to play a more important part in Gillian's life. They were just back from Guernsey in time to see the screening on BBC TV of the first in a new series of A Question of Sport. Henry Cooper and Fred Trueman were the team captains in those days, and in the few days between Philadelphia and St Peter Port, Gillian had recorded the show. Contrary to cynical public expectation, the quiz is not rehearsed and there is no dummy run. 'Light refreshment' at the Manchester studios and you're on, almost cold. The long-running and considerable success of the show is due not only to the director and producer, but to the happy confidence of the team captains — who before Gillian's next appearance had changed to Gareth Edwards and Emlyn Hughes.

A month after Guernsey and the lady was on the way to Indonesia again, for a fortnight of sunshine and exhibition matches that gave our old friends from the *Indonesia Times* a chance to exercise their English again: 'Verawaty really played groggy against the well-known English shuttler, who waved her racket and run up and down so well.' Again, the results were of no consequence, but it was no doubt a satisfying conclusion to this phenomenal season that Gillian did not lose a game in five singles matches. This little tour, which was staged to raise funds for a new hospital, was memorable less for the quality of the badminton than for the composition of the English party. Gillian was accompanied by two men: Mike Goodwin, the coach whose year of work with her had been so fruitful, and Mike Gilks, the husband whom she was about to leave. Her playing companion was 19-year-old Paula Kilvington, All-England junior champion in 1975 and now the fifth-ranked senior, who four years later became Gillian's doubles partner.

We have noted earlier the frenzied enthusiasm that greets badminton in Indonesia and there was a very clear example of the game's importance to the nation while the English party was there. The Indonesian men had just returned from winning the Thomas Cup in Bangkok, and President Suharto awarded the team bank deposits totalling 30 million rupeah (about £43,000). Rudy Hartono was given more than £7,000 and the rest of the team, including three coaches, each had half that sum. The deposit, said the President, was not meant to be a payment for their hard toil, but rather an incentive to keep the players in their profession(!) and encourage them to coach the younger generation to replace them when the time came. Another sample of Indonesian wealth and interest came at the end of the last match of the tour, when Gillian gave one of her rackets to be auctioned for charity: it fetched more than £700. The organisers capped that by auctioning Rudy Hartono's racket — for £1,800.

While Gillian Gilks was enjoying herself in Indonesia, Britain's leading male player, Paul Whetnall, was severing his connections with amateur badminton and with England. At the beginning of the year the Canadian Badminton Association advertised for a national coach, to live in Ottawa and travel extensively throughout the land for a salary of 15,000 dollars a year plus travel expenses. Whetnall got the job and started work in the summer. His wife, Sue, was to join him at the end of the year, which meant she would not be available to partner Gillian in defence of their All-England title. That was the start of something very big.

Gilks and Goodwin had been quoted, while they were in Indonesia, as suggesting that young Paula Kilvington would take Sue Whetnall's place as Gillian's doubles partner; but even if the quote was correct, it anticipated the event by four years. Gillian began the 1976–7 season playing with Barbara Giles (who later married Eddie Sutton), the 23-year-old Essex girl who had in her junior days enjoyed a successful partnership with Nora Gardner. With Miss Gardner now securely teamed with Maggie Lockwood, Miss Giles (an in-and-out member of the England squad) had not built another lasting doubles partnership. She had played the previous All-England with Mrs Nielsen, and the tie-up with Mrs Gilks made sense from England's viewpoint as well as from Gillian's. Gillian was clearly going to be a doubles force whoever she played with, and the England selectors were looking too for a replacement for Sue Whetnall.

According to Mrs Gilks, when Barbara wrote to her to ask if they could play together in the coming season, Gillian made it a condition of her agreement that

Mike Goodwin would coach and train both of them. Mrs Whetnall's vast experience and expertise at the doubles game, allied to that of Mrs Gilks, was such that the need for common coaching was never urgent, but much work had to be done on the Giles-Gilks combination. It didn't take long to get in the right groove: between mid-October and the end of November they won the Lincolnshire and Warwickshire Opens, and reached the final of the Highland and the Northumberland championships. This was despite the fact that Gillian had been troubled by a mysterious debility, later diagnosed as a kidney complaint. It forced her withdrawal from the international against West Germany, and from both doubles finals in the Northumberland, after she had lost the singles final to Mrs Lockwood.

The most important tournament in the first half of the season is always the English Nationals in December, a meeting at which Gillian Gilks had an astonishing history of success. She and Mrs Lockwood had held the singles title between them for eight years (four each); she had won the women's doubles four times in the previous five years, with three different partners; and she had only once failed to win the mixed doubles since 1967. Her hopes of a seventh successive mixed national title were severely damaged when Derek Talbot pulled out with an ankle injury on the day the competition began. Eddie Sutton partnered her to the final, where they lost in three to Tredgett and Gardner. Though Maggie Lockwood beat her in the singles final, Gilks and Giles had the immense satisfaction of beating England's leading pair, Gardner and Lockwood, in a three-game doubles final. It was the peak of their achievements, and the eve of their downfall.

After the Christmas break, during which Gillian received for the second time the Sportswoman of the Year award from the Sports Writers' Association, the first tournament of 1977 was the Swedish Open in Stockholm. It found Lene Koppen in irresistible mood — she easily beat both Lockwood and Gilks — but the doubles went very much England's way. Neither Talbot and Gilks nor Giles and Gilks lost a game in the whole tournament. That did not, alas, mean the passage was smooth. Anticipating a hard final against Gardner and Lockwood, coach Mike Goodwin had worked out a pattern of play that he wanted the girls to maintain throughout the competition. Faced with an absurdly easy match in the earlier stages, the pair failed to stick to the plan. Goodwin, who may not be the most tactful of men when roused, did not hesitate to tell them what he thought about it when they came off court.

Barbara Giles, it seems, did not take kindly to the criticism. They won the final well enough (Gardner and Lockwood were unaccountably beaten in their first match by the Canadians, Clarkson and Youngberg), but the following week Miss Giles did not turn up for their scheduled training session. Perhaps too hastily — Solomon himself would find it hard to adjudicate on these matters — Gillian decided that if her badminton harmony was going to be disturbed by a continuing disagreement between Miss Giles and their coach, the best thing for the well-being of her singles game would be to abandon that doubles partnership. Mrs Gilks then made what she later recognised as an unfortunate misjudgement in view of the delicacy of the

Seldom successful internationally, Ray Stevens has been five times the English National singles champion and, with Mike Tredgett, seven times the doubles champion

Maggie Lockwood (right) *and Nora Perry (formerly Gardner), who each won an All-England doubles title partnering Gillian, twice reached the final together*

situation. She did not tell Miss Giles of the decision herself, much less discuss it with her, but left it to her coach to inform Barbara that the partnership was ended.

There was one more match that they were committed to play together. Their earlier successes in Hearts of Oak tournaments had earned them a place in the circuit finals at Crystal Palace at the end of January. Gillian opened the evening with a devastating 14-minute win over Maggie Lockwood, 11–4, 11–0. After Derek Talbot had re-established his ascendancy over Ray Stevens, the Giles-Gilks crumbling team faced Mrs Lockwood and Miss Gardner (almost on the eve of her marriage to Joe Perry). They lost, heavily. As they walked off court it was obvious to spectators, if it had not been so earlier, that their unity had dissolved. According to a reporter at the courtside, Miss Giles turned to her partner and said: 'I don't want to talk to you ever again.' Mrs Gilks remembers the sentence as 'Do me a favour, never speak to me again,' but the details of the composition are overwhelmed by its fury. Barbara Giles told reporters that, until that night, Mrs Gilks had not spoken to her since the Swedish championships more than a fortnight earlier: 'I think that is rank bad manners and shows a total lack of ethics.'

By then Gillian had told the England selectors that the partnership was at an end, and that in future she wanted to play doubles with Anne Statt, a 22-year-old Hampshire player who was the All-England junior champion in 1974. This did not endear the lady to the BAE. Said Peter Birtwistle, chairman of the events committee: 'England teams will be picked by the selectors and no one else. You can take it from me that Mrs Gilks will not be playing in the women's doubles at next month's Dutch Open championships.'

You might think, if you were a reader outside the badminton world, that it could not be within the powers of even the BAE to dictate to an individual player in such absolute terms; and of course Gillian Gilks was at liberty to play doubles with anyone who was happy to play with her. But the BAE were also at liberty not to pick that partnership for an England team and, more significantly, not to nominate the partnership for tournaments at which the BAE controlled the entries. The Netherlands Association, for instance, would have presumably asked the BAE to nominate a certain number of singles and doubles players for the Dutch Open, whose expenses would be paid; and the BAE were not likely to nominate a pair whom they did not intend to select for international matches.

Two days later the BAE confirmed that they were putting the knife in by omitting Mrs Gilks from the women's doubles in Holland; and they twisted the blade. Barbara Giles was nominated to play with Jane Webster, fair enough; and Anne Statt, never before nominated by England, was entered with Paula Kilvington. In effect, it seemed from the outside as though the Association had said: 'No, you can't play with Anne Statt, she isn't good enough;' and had then eaten their own logic by including her in the squad. Gillian knew well that there was much more to worry about than missing one event of the Dutch Open (she was nominated for the singles and mixed). In May, only three months ahead, stood a golden goal: the first world badminton championships. Already the All-England titles made her the unofficial world champion. The summit of her current ambition was to add the official world title to her achievements, and she could see that war with the BAE could well result in her exclusion from that vital squad.

After the knife, the boot: the BAE events committee followed swiftly by reprimanding Mrs Gilks for wearing advertising insignia on court, and threatened her with suspension if the offence were repeated. This followed the incident we mentioned earlier, when she put on her track suit top while waiting for shuttles to be changed before the singles final at Crystal Palace. In the circumstances now prevailing between them, it was probably inevitable that the BAE should make the most and a bit more of another opportunity to damage Mrs Gilks. They informed her of their decision, she said, 'in the snottiest letter imaginable. It was disgraceful.' Reinforcing that earlier decision to exclude Gilks and Statt from the Dutch Open, the committee also publicly reminded anybody who cared to listen that the selectors could 'refuse permission for any player to play anywhere' if they felt it necessary.

Mrs Gilks could only reply by showing the Association what she was worth. She and Anne Statt proceeded to win the Essex Open, beating the selectors' choices of Jane Webster and Barbara Giles, and Nora Perry and Maggie Lockwood; the Durham Open, beating Webster and Giles again; and the Surrey Open. In Holland she retained her singles title and had the perverse satisfaction of seeing the nominated English pairs fail for the first time to win the women's doubles. At the end of February the BAE announced that they would not oppose the Gilks-Statt entry for the All-England, but asked Mrs Gilks to put on record that the official nomination was not acceptable to her. 'The situation is serious,' said selectors' chairman Ron Lockwood. 'We must now consider what it means in terms of the England team for international matches.' (You might think, as a mere observer, that what it meant was shown fairly clearly by the fact that Gilks and Statt had beaten at least once any other English pair that could be thrown against them. But there were complications: the Uber Cup team is restricted to six players, three of whom have to play singles and four of whom have to play doubles.)

Just one week later the BAE presented Gillian Gilks with an ultimatum: unless she gave them written assurance that she would abide by their nominations, she would not be considered for future England teams. She refused to do so, and was promptly dropped from the reckoning for the world championships. Mrs Gilks was not happy: 'I refuse to play under sufferance. For ten years I have given my best for England and have won more caps than all the selectors put together. The selectors have always given fair consideration to freely-formed partnerships with proven results, and there should be no complaints from those players without results.' In an earlier conversation with selector John Havers, he had made it clear to her that unless she agreed to play with Barbara Giles, she was out; but in making their announcement the BAE denied that they were trying to force Mrs Gilks to accept Miss Giles. As a result, in the middle of March, a compromise was reached. On the understanding that she would not be paired with Giles, and on Gillian's undertaking to make herself available to play against Japan in their tour of Britain after the All-England, the BAE said she would be in the team for the world championships in Malmo — but she would not be playing women's doubles with anyone.

By now the squabbling was attracting considerable attention in the national Press, which almost daily came out with the latest coughs and spits from one side or the other. In a substantial summing-up of the story so far in *The Observer*, I wrote at the time: 'The focus of the storm, a gentle blonde with a hard centre, shuffled through her involved file of correspondence for me again, painstakingly pointing out the propriety of her part in the affair of the unwelcome partner. It is a tedious business, close to being ridiculous; one of those absurd wrangles in which the establishment and a determined individual grow less transigent week by week.' Later in the piece I noted that 'Gillian Gilks, not a lady to bend with the wind, is now firmly established as the black sheep of the badminton family.' Quite right, she said three years later, they did look on me as a black sheep, and they still do. 'Everything I did then, I was in the wrong — the Indonesian business, the track suit top, Barbara Giles, Anne Statt, everything. Every step I took made me one step worse in their eyes, and they saw — see — Mike Goodwin as being behind it all, because they think he tells me what to do all the time. He is behind me, but he is the brick wall standing behind all I believe in. Without the wall behind me, I would have just given way, as I had always done in the past.'

Within a week of *The Observer* feature, the London *Evening News* devoted half a page to what Peter Batt called 'a conflict which is manufacturing unnecessary bitterness and seriously damaging the image of a game that has earned the reputation of the fastest-growing sport in the world.' Three days later the *Daily Express* were at it in force. Mrs Gilks, wrote James Lawton, 'has given her emerging minority sport the sort of publicity spurt Uri Geller once gave spoon-bending.' He got this interesting line out of Gillian: 'I accept the charge that perhaps I am pushing the game in England faster than it can comfortably go. But my attitude is that if I am prepared to make the sacrifice, take the time, I should be allowed certain rights. Like playing with the player of my choice. I think badminton can get a lot bigger, that there is an awful lot of scope, and I do resent the fact that I have to put up with what I can only describe as bureaucratic interference.'

With this appalling background, the perfect script for a badminton horror story, Gillian Gilks faced the defence of her historic three titles in the 1977 All-England — and for once it was almost more important that she (and Anne Statt) should do well in the doubles than that she should win the singles. Both partners were on record as saying that they were determined to win the title to show the BAE who should be in the England team. They didn't do badly — in the second round they beat Takada and Tokuda, who were to win the title the next year — but they lost to the seeded Indonesians Widiastuty and Regina Masli, 15–10, 12–15, 15–6. Of the other English pairs, only Mrs Lockwood and Mrs Perry got further: they beat the Indonesians in three games, losing the final to the Japanese pair, Toganoo and Ueno. There was, for sure, a certain amount of relief among the establishment that the rebels had not shown too great a hand — a Gilks-Statt victory would have been desperately embarrassing.

This year of 1977 was the one in which Flemming Delfs brought the All-England men's title back to Europe for only the second time in ten years, after a delightful and extremely close final with Liem Swie King. The women's semi-finals saw the old quartet of Koppen, Lockwood, Gilks and Yuki, and neither of the Britons survived, nor even won a game. Miss Yuki won her fourth singles crown, and the only British triumph was, again, that of Mrs Gilks and Derek Talbot, who maintained their mixed supremacy without being fully extended. Gillian looked and sounded tired by the end of the week — no doubt due to the emotional pressures as much as the physical — and would dearly have loved to shoot off on her Spanish holiday instantly. But the Japanese had to be faced first.

It was a four-match tour played in nine days at Torquay, Walsall, Newcastle and Preston, and considerably to their surprise, England took the series by three rubbers to one. The English selectors sensibly persisted with their chosen world championships women's pairs of Lockwood-Perry and Giles-Webster throughout the tour, and they lost only one of the eight matches they played. Gillian was called on for only two singles, losing to Tokuda and beating Kondo. Three weeks later they all went to Malmo and started all over again.

12 Outbreak of hostilities

If the relationship between Mrs Gilks and the Badminton Association had lost its amiability during the 1976–7 season, it became positively hostile during the 1977 summer, in which Gillian reached 27 years of age. It was preceded by the first world championships, in Sweden, in which she was taking part as a singles and mixed doubles player only. She had won every other meaningful title in the world, and this was her first and almost certainly her best chance to become an official world champion. At this stage in her career, nothing could have been more important.

The first four seeds in the women's singles were, as usual, Koppen and Yuki, Gilks and Lockwood, and there was never a great deal of chance that anybody would edge them out of their semi-final places. In the course of getting there, Yuki dropped one game to the German, Brigitte Steden, and Koppen narrowly lost one to Saori Kondo, but at no stage were either of them in danger of losing the match. Thanks to Joke van Beusekom's early defeat, Mrs Gilks reached her semi without meeting a seeded player, and was never in the slightest trouble. Not even Hiroe Yuki, the old enemy, was in shape to deflect her progress, and in 14 minutes Gillian Gilks was a world finalist. That was a performance of the very highest class, but it was one she could not repeat in the final against Lene Koppen. Once again, Mrs Gilks seemed ill at ease, but nevertheless it was no walkover for the Dane. They were neck and neck until Miss Koppen won the last three points of the first game to win 12–9; in the second Mrs Gilks caught up from 6–10 to lead at 11–10, but two unforced errors gave the match and the title to Koppen.

In other departments there was all kinds of excitement. Ray Stevens, drawn against joint top seed Flemming Delfs in the second round, played magnificently to take the first game 15–11. After the second went 15–10 to Delfs, there was the usual five-minute break. Delfs was nowhere in sight when the umpire indicated that the game should restart; three minutes later he came on court and saw the game and match awarded to Stevens. According to the *Daily Express*, 'Delfs waved his arms, stamped his feet and showed disgust. Although manager John Havers told Stevens to stay out of the row, the Englishman stepped forward and shouted: "I can't win like this. Let's play." ' The umpire allowed play to continue. Delfs took the game 15–6 and though he was within a whisker of losing his next match to Kinji Zeniya, of

Japan, he just survived and did not lose another game in the tournament.

Politics showed up, too. Because of the presence of a New Zealander, Brian Purser, the four Zambian male competitors were withdrawn from the tournament. Purser was beaten in the first round, so back came the Zambians. They were all beaten in the first round too. Meanwhile, in the background, the International Badminton Federation were meeting. Though China's application for membership was kept pending, they did at last vote to exclude Taiwan.

Back on court, Stevens and Tredgett did very well to reach the semi-finals at the expense of the seeded Danes, Delfs and Skovgaard, but the final was all-Indonesian. The women's doubles, alas, brought no such joy to the English players or their selectors. Top-seeded Lockwood and Perry lost in the semi-final to a Dutch pair, van Beusekom and Ridder-Luesken, and the controversial coupling of Giles and Webster, seeded 3–4, lost in their first match. The most surprising success in the mixed was that of the talented Scots, Billy Gilliland and Joanna Flockhart, who reached the semis by beating two seeded pairs, the second of which were David Eddy and Barbara Giles. Eddie Sutton and Jane Webster went down in the first round to Canadians, and top-seeded Mike Tredgett and Nora Perry did not survive the semi-final. Skovgaard and Koppen proved their undoing, and the Danes were also too good in the final for Talbot and Gilks, 15–12, 18–17.

There was a rare display of emotional aggression in this match, after Talbot had twice seen shots called out by the same linesman, when he was sure they were in. On the second occasion he crossed the net to confront the official before protesting to the umpire, who asked the linesman to leave the court. Overall, it was a disappointing championships for the English, who saw three titles go to Denmark, one to Japan and one to Indonesia.

That was the end of badminton until September, but not the end of arguments nor, for Mrs Gilks, the end of physical activity. She was committed, the very next day, to take part in the first female 'Superstars' competition for television. The organisers had hoped that she (with Mike Goodwin) would have been able to catch the 5.30 p.m. ferry from Malmo to Copenhagen, and the 7.0 flight to Heathrow, the last one there was on that Sunday. Gillian's participation in the mixed doubles final made that impossible, and Trans World International, the company that organises and stages 'Superstars' for television, had to arrange a private plane to fly them that evening from Malmo direct to Stansted airport, in Essex. That would have been no hardship, except that the cabin heater packed up during the flight. All the blankets and top coats that could be found were massed around them, but by the time they landed at midnight it was hard to believe it was Spring.

The night in a Huntingdonshire hotel was all too short: at 6.30 she was roused to undergo a safety procedure test in a swimming pool to ensure she would survive if her canoe overturned. By lunchtime she had competed twice and was lying fourth. She opted out of swimming (handsomely won by water-skier Karen Morse), came fourth in canoeing (athletes Donna Murray and Ann Brightwell were well ahead) and won the basketball shooting with nine baskets within the minute. As Gillian is badly affected by height, she opted out of the first day's gymnastic test too: 'I couldn't possibly walk along a beam. I couldn't even stand on it, not without something to hold on to. I can look out of a very high window all right, as long as there's a rail there. If there's just a low rail round an open balcony or something, I would have to go down on my knees to look over — I must be in contact with something solid. When we were in China, I climbed quite high up one of the towers in the Great Wall and that was all right, but when we turned round to come down I almost had a fit. I had to get Elliot Stuart to walk in front of me and I put my hands on his shoulders the whole way down.'

Despite only taking part in two of the four competitions, Gillian still ended the day in fourth place. Donna Murray had a clear lead, having won the gym as well as the canoeing, but (unable to take part in either of the running events) scored no points at all on the second day. That opened with a hockey dribbling test, in which Gillian was second to the former skiing star Davina Galica; then the 100 metre sprint (fourth, won by Ann Brightwell) and the cycling (third). With one event to go, the 400 metre run, Ann Brightwell had 32 points, but wasn't competing again; Davina Galica had 31; Karen Morse had 30, but she wasn't running; and Gillian had 25. With ten points for the winner, seven for the runner-up and four for third place in each event, only Gilks and Galica could overtake Brightwell. Gillian had to win the 400 to do it, but even if she did, Davina Galica could beat her by coming second. Gillian did win, Miss Galica was fourth, and Gillian collected £1,000 — well worth a hectically tiring few days. It was not altogether surprising that she should win, for there couldn't have been much doubt that, all-round, she was the fittest woman there. What was unexpected, and even embarrassing, was the poor performance by the youngest competitor, 19-year-old cycling star Denise Burton, who only managed to secure eight points from her six events.

A few weeks later, towards the end of June 1977, the Badminton Association announced a radical and unexpected change in the selection structure. The selection committee, whose work in the previous year had not led to much triumph, was no more. Following the example of association football and tennis, player selection and management was to be the sole responsibility of one person; Judy Hashman, with the assistance of coach Maurice Robinson. Such an appointment is usually not agreed without controversy, noted Richard Streeton in *The Times*:

> 'It can only be surmised, however, that a feeling has prevailed that Mrs Hashman's character, inspirational force and stature as a player would stand the best chance to direct England's efforts singlemindedly at international level. She would be better placed, too, as an individual to solve any personality clashes which might arise. Some people believe these have prevented England players from doing themselves justice on international occasions in the past.'

Streeton made another equally surprising disclosure in the same story: Gillian Gilks would not be available to play for England in the Uber Cup. When this news came out, it was generally supposed in the game that the decision could not be divorced from her pique at the BAE refusing to bless her doubles partnership with Anne Statt. But as *The Times* man so precisely put it, Mrs Gilks 'found that economically it was not practical to commit her life to badminton without more financial help.' That help, she hoped, would come from a sports shop that she and Mike Goodwin were about to open in a terrace close to the railway station at New Barnet, a Hertfordshire suburb a few miles up the line from King's Cross. It was not the smartest of sites. Previously a restaurant and then a wool shop, it had been unoccupied for more than a year. The skylight was broken, there were pigeons in the loft and water had come through the bedroom ceiling. But it was not an expensive lease, as a High Street pitch would have been. With the unstinted help of gangs of local badminton players, as well as visiting players from the United States, New Zealand and Spain, gallons of paint and plaster were applied through the summer and the shop, Champion Sports, opened in September 1977.

It was clear from the outset that running the business (Goodwin, an architect, had his own business to run) was going to interfere with the all-out badminton onslaught that Gillian had been accustomed to conducting. The shop was not large enough to support full-time staff, but she hoped it would provide the security she needed after the break-up of her marriage, as well as being a financial prop. At that time, man could not live on badminton alone. 'I knew I would have to be selective about the badminton I played once the shop was open. It seemed to me the best thing to do was to stay out of the England representative events and just play the occasional individual tournament when I could arrange part-time help in the shop. I mean, I'd got to the age when, in my circumstances, I had to be thinking about my future after badminton.'

Racket sports were to form the basis of the business, but Mrs Gilks soon found the turnover in footwear was so large it was worth stocking up with trainers and football boots, and all the clothing that went with the sports. 'The business ticked over quite nicely, but it needed more time and energy than we gave it. Initially I saw it as something stable, dependable, but in the end it became almost as much hassle as the badminton. With the paperwork, you could quite well be working from eight in the morning to ten at night, but despite the headaches I enjoyed it. Perhaps living over the shop wasn't a good idea — you never left the job — but when the accommodation is there what else can you do? I would love to have worked at it full-time and expanded the business, but without giving up badminton altogether that wasn't possible.' After two years they sold the shop: open badminton had by then arrived, with its appealing financial possibilities. But in the summer of 1977 that was not a consideration.

On July 1st, Judy Hashman wrote to all the leading female players, calling them to a meeting to discuss the Uber Cup and other international fixtures. Gillian's intentions were by then known, and she replied declining the invitation and explaining that, because of her business commitments, she would rather not be considered for international selection. The secretary of the BAE, Brian Bisseker, told the Press: 'Mrs Gilks has declined even to meet the new selectors. She has stated that she does not wish to take part in any discussions, nor to be present at a special meeting between the new selectors at Reading.' Not surprisingly, the nature if not the fact of the Gilks refusal was considered rather churlish. Judy Hashman was reported to be 'bitterly disappointed' and Maurice Robinson was worse: 'If Gillian wants to change her mind and play, Judy and I would be delighted. But we're not going to be messed around. If anyone says no, now, then that means no. She can't come to us in six months' time and say she wants to come in again.'

Nick Budibent, the BAE's development and publicity officer, was responsible for setting up a private meeting between Mrs Hashman and Mrs Gilks at the end of August, at which Gillian was able to explain her personal and business problems in detail, and at which she said she hoped that when the shop was running efficiently she would be able to come back to international badminton. 'I thought,' said Gillian, 'that Judy had understood all that. She said she would put the outcome down on paper, and two days later I had a letter from her saying she was pleased I had agreed to make myself available for the following internationals — and she listed just about everything on the calendar.'

Between them, the two parties had once again failed to understand each other, failed to communicate. The result was another letter, from Gilks to Hashman, in which she returned to her stance of not playing for England at all 'rather than be accused of picking and choosing what I will or won't do.' And so, grimly and with little good humour, the 1977–8 season got under way. The women's ranking list, issued during the summer, was of particular interest. Gilks and Lockwood were named joint top, followed by the next generation: Jane Webster, Paula Kilvington, Karen Bridge, Anne Statt. (Nora Perry was in action too, but had not played enough singles the previous season to be ranked.) Though there was an interesting depth of talent, it was promising rather than tested; and the Uber Cup selection began to be positively worrying without Gilks and in the knowledge that Maggie Lockwood had just had a cartilage operation on her right knee.

Mrs Gilks was not left long in doubt as to the problems she was going to have to face. As a private preliminary to the season, she and Anne Statt went over for the Vaerlose tournament in Denmark in the middle of September. Gillian lost an extraordinary final to Lene Koppen (11–0, 0–11, 11–2), and the English pair won the doubles. That was the last time she was able to play with Mrs Statt. The BAE told Anne to cease her partnership with Gillian if she wanted to remain in the England squad. By then the Association had withdrawn from Gillian what might reasonably be regarded as her right to defend her title in the English Invitation singles. They did so, according to their statement, 'so that another lady has an opportunity to prove her worth'. Secretary Larry Landrey responded to the fuss in the national Press by saying: 'I can't help feeling this has all been blown up out of all proportion.' But at the same time, without even informing the lady, the BAE were diverting personal invitations to her (sent via their office) to play in tournaments in Denmark and India.

Their next move was an unusually vicious one: the BAE changed Rule 3c of their regulations so that registered players, as well as amateurs, were forced to seek the Association's approval before playing anywhere abroad. Almost before the ink had dried on that amended rule, wrote Brian James in the *Daily Mail*, the BAE used it to refuse Mrs Gilks permission to play in all or any of the five foreign tournaments she had earmarked as preparation for defending her three European titles in April. Hard words passed between solicitors on both sides, one of whom was using phrases like 'restraint of trade' and 'infringement of individual rights', and the other was concocting patriotic clauses about the Association being only concerned to do the best for England and its teams. The reason for changing Rule 3c was merely an administrative convenience, they said, and had nothing at all to do with the Gilks situation. It was not surprising that did not impress Mrs Gilks: in her file she had a smuggled copy of the relevant committee minute. It mentioned her by name and made it clear that the rule was changed precisely to close a loophole so that she could be banned from travel.

Judy Hashman ferociously defended the Association's moves to the *Mail* man. It would be the worst possible thing for English team morale, she said, if Mrs Gilks were to go to an overseas tournament privately and hammer one of the English team members in front of foreign rivals. 'And it's damn bad for morale to have someone around who is prepared to travel to a tournament for herself and her sponsors' contracts, but not for her country.' It was clear, wrote Brian James, that these two ladies were never going to love each other again.

Meanwhile, what was happening on the domestic front? Mrs Lockwood was still on the injured list and Paula Kilvington won the Invitation Singles without conceding a game. Not unexpectedly, Mrs Gilks swept through the Northumberland singles, the Northern singles, the Welsh singles and the English Nationals. The last was her fifth National singles win and her eleventh consecutive final. Other members of the English team were swept aside disdainfully — Nora Perry, the finalist, only survived for ten minutes and the first game, 11–0, lasted three minutes and 40 seconds. But the doubles, they produced different problems. Gillian did not contest the women's doubles in any of those tournaments, in which the officially-nominated pairs were Mrs Perry with Mrs Statt, Mrs Sutton (formerly Barbara Giles) with Miss Webster — or permutations of the same four.

She entered the Northumberland mixed with Elliot Stuart, and saw the selectors promptly remove Stuart, a former English international, to partner someone else. He declined, and with Gillian won the Northumberland, the Northern and the Welsh. (Why no Derek Talbot, Gillian's traditional and brilliant partner? In all those tournaments he contested, and often won, the singles and men's doubles, but he was not at that stage in the season playing any mixed.) So, not yet beaten in singles and only once in mixed — the National final — she had nothing to complain of in her results for the first half of the season. And there was better news to come. In mid-

In 1978, at full stretch, Gillian Gilks won the All-England singles title for the second time, ecstatically beating Saori Kondo (Japan) in the final

The old master and the new: the legendary Rudy Hartono (left), *eight-times All-England champion, gave way to his Indonesian colleague Liem Swie King at Wembley in 1978. But Hartono was still good enough to win the world title two years later*

December the BAE executive committee conceded that they had been wrong in banning Mrs Gilks from overseas play. Undoubtedly reflecting the widespread feeling among other players, they issued a firm directive to the events committee to free her. The decision, said Nick Budibent, 'is the result of some serious lobbying on Mrs Gilks' behalf, both from inside the Association and from outside. She has many supporters.'

Overdue though that decision was (it was not ratified until the events committee met in January), it had to be interpreted as a waving of the olive branch. Gillian was able to compete in the Dutch Open, where she retained her singles title and reached the final of the women's doubles with a new partner, Mrs Pauline Ferrington (they were beaten by Nora Perry and Anne Statt). A fortnight later, releasing her own dove, she stressed to a reporter of the London *Evening News* that she was seeking conciliation and not confrontation with the BAE. She was careful not to blame Mrs Hashman for their misunderstanding in the summer, and expressed the hope that she might play for England again the following season, 'if they will have me back.' Then there was a cry for more doves and more olives: 'I am so conscious of the need not to upset people that I am not even sure how I will go about making myself available again.'

Many of us hoped that sense and sympathy and sweetness and light would gently return to the scene from that moment, but such peaceful hopes were harshly extinguished during the final day of the 1978 All-England championships at Wembley, in a dressing-room corridor conversation that led the reporter of *The Observer* to state: 'It is now a dead certainty that Mrs Gilks will not be invited to represent England again.' These were the championships in which Rudy Hartono capitulated in an unbelievable final to Liem Swie King, having quite marvellously beaten, in succession, Sture Johnsson, Morton Frost Hansen and Flemming Delfs. The old wizard was playing so well that some at the courtside believed he had never been better. Yet, in the final, he allowed himself to slump from 10–7 up in the first game to 0–8 down in the second without winning a point. It was not credible, and when Swie King, through his tears of joy after the match, suggested that Hartono had let him win, one was not exactly deafened by the protests of his listeners.

There were some surprising goings-on in the women's doubles, not the least of which was that the committee chose to seed Mrs Gilks and Mrs Ferrington rather than the Uber Cup pairing of Mrs Sutton and Miss Webster. The latter underlined the point by beating the impressive Japanese partnership of Hiroe Yuki and Saori Kondo. Mrs Gilks and her partner lost to the eventual champions, Tokuda and Takada; at the other end of the draw the joint top seeds, Mrs Perry and Mrs Statt, had a most uncomfortable time, aggravated by a leg injury to Mrs Statt. They only just scraped home against Verawaty and Wigoeno, the Indonesians who were to win the title the following year, and were then put out by the unseeded Canadians, Backhouse and Youngberg. The mixed was clouded by another misunderstanding: Derek Talbot had apparently played no mixed doubles all the season, so Gillian entered with Svend Pri. Talbot, who hoped to be going for a hat-trick with her, was shocked. He entered with young Karen Puttick (now Karen Chapman), and they lost to Pri and Gilks in the quarter-finals. Mike Tredgett and Nora Perry took the title for the first time, beating Pri and Gilks with difficulty and Skovgaard and Koppen easily.

And the women's singles? Gillian Gilks won, for the second time, and oddly enough there was never much doubt that she was going to do so. She blazed through to the semis, where Hiroe Yuki awaited. Hiroe Yuki, greatest of all Japanese, who had beaten her in the 1974 and 1975 finals, and in the 1977 semi-final; a player who, unlike some of her compatriots, retained both physical and mental toughness to the last shot of the match. Though Gillian looks back on this match as one of her most memorable achievements, it was a curiously uneven performance. She took the first game 12–11 after saving a game point, lost the second 11–5 almost casually, and then romped through the third with what Richard Streeton in *The Times* called 'an abruptness that was both majestic and ruthless.' The last eight points were hers without argument. Miss Yuki, the holder, was out. If seeding had been followed, Gillian would have faced Lene Koppen again, but the world champion had not even reached the semi-finals, being beaten by Canada's Wendy Clarkson. She fell to Saori Kondo, who was not ready for an All-England singles final. In the first game she had little to offer but confusion and went down 11–1 in six minutes in the face of some devastating badminton. She came out for the next, I noted in *The Observer*, 'less like a lamb than a Samurai warrior. She attacked so successfully that Gilks netted two backhands for 1–1, changed her racket, netted two forehands for 2–1 and changed two more rackets before reaching 2–2. At 4–5 down she tossed aside another racket in a way that must have made her equipment sponsor sweat a little.' The sponsor was Sondico, who may not have sweated, but certainly bridled. In their next monthly newsletter this paragraph appeared: 'Sondico wish to point out that the trouble Mrs Gilks had with her rackets during the match was due to stringing by an independent company, and not due in any way to faults in the frame, as mistakenly reported by Press and commentators.'

Gillian won the second game 11–9, and soon afterwards was, to her surprise, approached outside the Wembley dressing-room by Judy Hashman: would Gillian let bygones be bygones and play in the Uber Cup European final against Denmark? She was given half an hour to make her decision, but she didn't take it. It would have been a splendidly generous gesture to have said 'yes' and to have flung her arms round the formidable frame of Mrs Hashman, who had earlier banned Gilks from internationals as surely as Gillian had refused them. Gillian did neither. It just might have made life lovely again to this very minute, it could have avoided three more years of aggravation, but it would have been inconsistent. Mrs Gilks is seldom that. She had said from the first, no Uber Cup, and no Uber Cup it was going to be. Somewhere within the castle of international badminton a mighty door slammed shut, and the sound has echoed gloomily through the corridors ever since.

13 Money and more money

Just three weeks later Judy Hashman was sacked as the badminton supremo. With the most extraordinarily provocative sense of timing, the Badminton Association made this decision known on the eve of the European Championships at Preston, Lancashire. Mrs Hashman's one-year contract — embracing selection, team managership and non-playing captaincy of all national teams — was due to expire (though with the expectation of renewal) on June 30th, with the additional understanding that she would be responsible for the August Commonwealth Games in Canada. The BAE decided, without warning or rumour, that the Commonwealth Games selection should be in the hands of a committee of five, of which Mrs Hashman was invited to be a member under the chairmanship of John Havers. Of course she declined the invitation, and her term of office (together with that of coach Maurice Robinson) was cut abruptly short: she was to hand over at the end of the European Championships.

By the time she received her notice, England were out of the Uber Cup, having lost to Denmark, and after the bi-sexual Commonwealth Games the next major international event was the Thomas Cup, the men's team competition. 'It would have been very difficult for Mrs Hashman to remain,' said Peter Birtwistle, tournament director for the European Championships. 'There had been too many complaints coming in from our foreign trips. There were rows everywhere she went.' Not unexpectedly, Mrs Hashman was 'very hurt', and felt the BAE had pulled the carpet from under her feet. On the last day of the Europeans she made a final, pointless gesture: she fulfilled the terms of her contract by handing to the Association her chosen team for the Commonwealth Games, a copy of which she sent to the English Commonwealth Games Council. The BAE, of course, cancelled it; but at least Mrs Hashman had the satisfaction, a month later, of seeing them officially announce the same team.

Gillian Gilks was in neither the Commonwealth Games team, which would have been impossible to equate with her business commitments, nor in the team at Preston, which regained the team championship against Denmark despite Derek Talbot and Jane Webster being ruthlessly demolished in the two singles matches. Talbot lasted two games and 22 minutes against Delfs, Webster two games and 16 minutes against Koppen, both predictable defeats. The three doubles pairs splendidly saved the day for England. There was not much sense, after that, in laying a bet against the same two Danes to win the individual titles, which they duly did. It was a pleasant surprise that Miss Webster beat Joke van Beusekom to reach the singles final, where she fought doughtily against Miss Koppen for two games and collapsed in the third. The doubles story was, as usual, a happier one: Stevens and Tredgett retained their title, Nora Perry and Anne Statt secured the women's doubles, Tredgett and Perry took the mixed — a conclusion that could only have been more satisfactory if either Mrs Gilks or Mrs Lockwood had been playing.

Other than the back-stage rumblings, there was only one unfortunate incident, summarised in the headline in *The Times* after the first day's play: 'Jolly loses game, temper and interest in match'. The stormy young Essex player, Kevin Jolly, on whom placidity has never sat easily nor for long, blew his top after disputing several line calls, the last of which cost him the first game, 18–17 to Jesper Helledie (Denmark). According to Richard Streeton, Jolly then threw his racket to the floor with considerable force, stamped his foot, shouted loudly at the linesman and threw the next game away 15–1. 'A most foolish demonstration,' said Peter Birtwistle. 'It won't end here.' Despite his written apology, Jolly was within hours sent home in disgrace and was later officially reprimanded — but not suspended, thus allowing him to take his expected place in the team for Edmonton. In those 1978 Games, the singles titles went to Prakash Padukone (who beat Talbot in the final) and Sylvia Ng of Malaysia. Nora Perry partnered Anne Statt (who had just become Anne Skovgaard) and Mike Tredgett to two more doubles championships. That meant that in the space of five months the Tredgett-Perry partnership had taken the All-England, European and Commonwealth mixed doubles titles.

All in all, it was a heck of a lively 'off-season'. Throughout the year, international politics had been rampant in the game. The People's Republic of China, tired of having their conditional applications to join the International Badminton Federation turned down (the condition always being that Taiwan was excluded) had backed the formation of a breakaway body, the World Badminton Federation. Predictably, this had been fiercely outlawed by the IBF, and among its Eastern adherents it had not attracted Indonesia or Japan, who faced expulsion from the Uber and Thomas Cups if they joined. Running parallel with this move came the Badminton Players' Association, who felt that the BAE, not to mention the IBF, were dragging their feet about organising open badminton. The BPA, whose members included most of the leading players of the Western World at least, had been making alarming noises about finding an entrepreneur to set up with them an international circuit to stage big-money badminton, and some response had apparently come from Mark McCormack, the millionaire American sports manager and promoter. To the BPA, the formation of the new WBF could have led to such a circuit, with the ultimate dream of China facing the rest of the world on coast-to-coast American television with fortunes made all round.

Neither the BAE nor the IBF were anxious to see all their greatest players ripped off in one rush for the money. The BAE were in principle committed to the open game, but were understandably reluctant to go for it without the sanction and encouragement of the IBF — who still insisted on the limit of £100 prize money for the winner of any event. The IBF would perhaps have moved a little faster but for their hope that badminton would be accepted as an Olympic sport in 1984. The Olympic dreams had long been cherished by the badminton world (it had been a demonstration sport at the 1972 Games), but a professional camp within the sport would dampen the chance of those dreams becoming reality, and the existence of two world governing bodies would drown it. Eventually the IBF, in May 1978, accepted a resolution from England that affiliated national associations should be allowed to adopt open badminton after the next IBF meeting in May 1979. Motions from Canada and Sweden calling for instant open badminton were defeated, and the Players' Association, while welcoming the IBF move, were fairly peevish that they had to wait another whole season before laying their hands on real money.

With the open game now assured, Gillian Gilks could take a fresh look at her future plans. At the age of nearly 28, she could almost certainly earn more money from open badminton, at least for two or three years, than her shop seemed likely to provide. It was clearly judicious to re-establish reasonably harmonious relations with the new BAE regime. In July 1978 she declared her limited availability for England, and sent to John Havers her proposed programme for the following season. The rejections and compromises that followed did not produce a mutually agreeable scheme until Christmas. Meanwhile, Mrs Gilks had some gall-swallowing to do at the end of August, when the BAE announced the payment of training support grants of altogether £8,000 to its leading players. The list did not include Gillian, which was probably small surprise, but it did include Margaret Lockwood. Mrs Lockwood's determination and will to play for England again was never in doubt, but it was a fact that she was facing a third operation to her right knee, with only slight hope of ever being able to play international badminton again. Mrs Gilks was eventually accepted as an international player again and in the New Year received a grant from the BAE of £375.

As a prelude to the 1978–79 season, Gillian went to Australia (with Jane Webster and Ray Stevens) for three major tournaments. The trip brought sunshine and smiles and victory in the Australian Open in both singles and doubles (but subsequent singles defeat, for the first time, by the rising Indonesian star Wiharjo Verawaty). The success of Mrs Gilks' partnership with Miss Webster raised another possibility for the future, but the women's doubles scene in England was currently more confusing than usual. The marriage of Anne Statt to Skeen Skovgaard effectively broke up the leading pair, Perry and Statt, as a long-term prospect. Gillian, at the time, declined to take her place, which would have been a neat and tidy and no doubt triumphant solution. Mrs Gilks played (and won) the Northern with Marjan Ridder, of Holland, and the Nationals with Jane Webster; Mrs Perry won the Laing circuit with Barbara Sutton, but managed to play the All-England and several other tournaments with Anne Skovgaard.

One of the results of Mrs Gilks' choppy passage over the waters of badminton that year was that she should not be invited to take part in the Evening of Champions staged at Wembley in October. That the All-England champion, who had just been ranked the world's best by *World Badminton* was not there was ludicrous, but entirely predictable. The women's singles was between Lene Koppen, world and European champion, and Sylvia Ng of Malaysia, the Commonwealth Games winner, who had never beaten either Miss Koppen or Mrs Gilks. Gillian commentated on television for that event and did not play a domestic tournament until November, when she defended her Northern titles at Birkenhead. She won all three, happily returning to her mixed partnership with Derek Talbot, and then in December saved a match point in her English Nationals final against Nora Perry. After a brief and not entirely successful tour in Japan (she has never had a really good one there) came the news that the 18-month breach between Gillian Gilks and the BAE had been healed.

'We can forget what happened and look to the future', said Gillian. And selectors' chairman John Havers seemed equally sanguine: with Gillian partnering Nora Perry, he said, England could prepare for the World Championship and Uber Cup campaigns with confidence: 'I think both sides have made mistakes and hopefully both have learned from them. Gillian's shop is well-established now, she has a secure financial base, and generally is a much more settled person than she was.'

Even though such optimism may have rung rather hollowly in her ears, Gillian shot off to Holland and won all three titles in the Dutch Open, beating Lene Koppen 12–10, 12–9 and partnering Mrs Ridder and Derek Talbot in the doubles. In February she played her first game for England for two years, against Canada at Crawley, and in March she must have been slightly surprised to see herself seeded for the All-England below both Lene Koppen and Hiroe Yuki — presumably because of her lack of tournament play in the preceding year. The bookmakers, however, paid her the compliment of quoting her as 5–2 favourite to retain the singles title — not very generous odds for the punters when Widiastuty (Indonesia), Yonekura (Japan) and Wendy Carter of Canada, who the previous year had put out Lene Koppen, were all in her quarter, and Koppen was likely to be there for the semi-final. As usual, things didn't go exactly as anticipated. In the women's singles, Nora Perry (seeded) lost in the first round, but the biggest surprise of all was Jane Webster's win over Hiroe Yuki to reach the semis, giving England two chances of a finalist. They lost them both.

Miss Webster faced Saori Kondo with the psychological advantage of having beaten her in Glasgow the previous week, when Europe and Asia tied at five rubbers each. This time she began with equally immaculate control, leading 8–3 in the first, but when the Japanese (unseeded, despite being 1978 runner-up) began leaping for her smashes like a muscular firecracker, Jane began to falter. The match was over in

20 minutes. Gillian Gilks had one of her sad, sad matches that Friday evening. Undoubtedly tired after a heavy schedule the previous night (the penalty she always pays for contesting every event), she offered only a shadow of her brilliance in a performance laden with errors and misjudgements. So Koppen and Kondo, neither of whom had won the title before, met to contest it. It went to the Danish world champion, but only after a nasty fright: she lost the second game 11–1 in five minutes and sank to 5–0 in the third, but pulled it out of the fire 11–8. The crowd thereupon rose to their darling, who had taken the title to Denmark for the first time since 1953. *The Observer* noted that something was missing from the finals: 'Gillian Gilks, who achieved only the excellent by losing in all three semi-finals. That, by her extraordinary standards, rates as a disaster'. In the women's doubles, Gilks and Mrs Ridder, of the Netherlands, reached the semis, where they had a three-game battle with the eventual champions, Verawaty and Wigoeno; in the mixed the same thing happened to Gilks and Talbot, who lost a magnificent semi to Christian and Wigoeno 11–15, 17–14, 18–14. In the other half, Tredgett and Perry comfortably reached their appointed place in the final,where they lost 15–1, 18–17. That was the first time the All-England mixed doubles title had ever gone to Indonesia, the first time it had gone outside Europe since an American pair won it 30 years earlier, and the first time for seven years it had been taken away from England. Indonesia's winning of every title but the women's singles represented by far their greatest success at an All-England tournament.

During the season the badminton world — or at least the vast base of the pyramid — were considerably shocked to learn that random drug tests were to be held at the All-England, the first time in the history of the sport that such a thing were to happen. Even those of us who were cynically familiar with the sight of pepped-up athletes in other sports found it hard to accept that there was a chance that in badminton the worst could happen. Those closer to the dressing-rooms had a harder view of such matters and British players in general had long believed that the Indonesians sometimes took drugs. There was no proof, but their style of play was notoriously more aggressive than most others and there were times in Jakarta when every one of the Indonesians seemed to be playing above himself — the 1975 Uber Cup, for instance, when each girl was at the peak of her capability. They did seem to be 'high.' The five-minute rest period before a third game, introduced in 1975, undoubtedly made the matter of administering stimulants easier. As Richard Streeton wrote in *The Times*: 'It is a common sight in some countries to see a wilting player rushed to the secrecy of the dressing-room by a bevy of handlers during the break and return with energy to burn.'

The agreement of players to be checked for artificial stimulants after their matches was made a condition of entry to the All-England in 1979, and the BAE admitted the possibility that in future years they might also test for the presence of body-building drugs. If ever an end were abruptly to be made to the 'vicarage garden party' image of the sport, this was it; but so far, to general relief, no sinners have been found — or if they have, the authorities have kept quiet about it.

Another badminton sin caused a rumpus during the semi-finals of the men's doubles in 1979. Tjun Tjun and Wahjudi, the Indonesian holders of the title, were engaged in a tremendous battle with a Japanese pair, Iino and Tsuchida. At 15–6, 14–17 came the five-minute break, and the Indonesians disappeared to the dressing-room (as many do). They had only just re-entered the arena, and were some way from their court, when they heard umpire Alan Jones disqualify them for exceeding the statutory interval. The Indonesians protested mildly, the crowd protested with thunderous uprising (you'd be surprised how many Indonesians work in London) and almost immediately Herbert Scheele, the vastly-experienced referee, walked on court to overrule the umpire, whom he replaced. It was by no means the only time there has been such an incident (remember Ray Stevens and Flemming Delfs), but no other has produced such spirited and anxious reaction. 'It seems to me,' wrote one correspondent to the *Badminton Gazette*, 'there is a most serious point of principle at stake that must be decided very quickly by the IBF: under what circumstances, if at all, may a correct decision by an umpire be over-ruled by the referee?'

The same issue of the magazine carried a full-page feature on the subject. The author pointed out that Law 21 was unambiguous in stating 'there shall be an interval not exceeding five minutes'. Though common-sense might say 'What do a few seconds matter?', the umpire has no more right to bend that rule than he has to permit a toe to go one millimetre over the line. The referee may overrule him on a point of law, but the umpire is the sole arbiter of fact. As a subsequent letter from Alan Jones himself testified, every responsible effort had been made to warn the Indonesians, repeatedly, that the break was nearly at an end. Short of leading them by the hand back to their court, it is hard to see what else could have been done. But why, except in tropical countries, do we need a break at all? The *Gazette* writer was of no doubt that it was unnecessary: 'For the players, the break may be a restful interlude. But it is one in which rhythm can be lost and nerves become edgy. The player (or pair) who won the second game is held in check, loses, perhaps, his winning edge and his moral superiority, while his opponent thankfully seeks counsel, aid and sanctuary for five long minutes'. As another letter writer had it, the circumstances of that particular case were merely incidental to the crux of the matter, which was that the break meant fitness was no longer paramount. If you could last two games, you could recharge your batteries before facing the third: 'Surely the best badminton player is one who is fitter, stronger, quicker and more knowledgeable than the other. Are we not, by this ruling, perhaps preventing the best players from proving that they are the best?'

The conclusion of the All-England tournament meant that the BAE had once again to produce their list of the best, the annual domestic ranking list, and further controversy was highlighted. No question that Gillian Gilks should retain her Number 1 spot, but there was considerable surprise that Nora Perry was preferred to Jane Webster in second place: after all, Jane had beaten Mrs Perry in the final of the

(above) *Nora Perry and Jane Webster, 1980 world champions*

(right) *Nora Perry and Mike Tredgett, All-England, European and Commonwealth champions*

(left) *Svend Pri (Denmark), All-England champion in 1975*

(left below) *Prakash Padukone (India), 1980 All-England champion*

(below) *Lene Koppen (Denmark), former world, European and All-England champion*

(right) *Tjun Tjun and Wahjudi (Indonesia), six times All-England champions*

(left) *Wiharjo Verawaty (Indonesia), 1980 world champion*

(below) *Morten Frost Hansen (Denmark), European runner-up*

Laing Grand Prix, had taken Lene Koppen to three games in the semi-final of the Dutch Open, and had reached the semis in the All-England. Furthermore, as one of Miss Webster's vociferous supporters said, it was a bit much that she and Mrs Gilks should be ranked in the doubles equal second with Mrs Perry and Mrs Sutton (Mrs Perry and Mrs Skovgaard were first), when they had crushed them in less than 15 minutes to win the English Nationals. However, it remains impossible for any selectors to please all the players at once. The new young male star of British badminton, Kevin Jolly, was highly displeased at about this time, not with his position in the rankings (second equal with Derek Talbot), but because he was not invited to take part in badminton's first open tournament at the Albert Hall in September. Ray Stevens and Talbot were England's two singles representatives (to play for a £3,000 prize), and Jolly had beaten them both during the 1978–79 season — Talbot twice. It was not unreasonable of the selectors to stick to Talbot, who had given long and excellent service to England for very little reward. Jolly had plenty of time to enjoy the fruits of open badminton; and it was Jolly who, only a year earlier, had been sent home from the European championships for his court tantrums. And it was Jolly — though this was probably irrelevant — who memorably let slip a vital Thomas Cup match in the European Zone semi-final against Sweden. Playing the third singles when the match score was three-all, Jolly led Stefan Karlsson 15–11 and 13–8. Despite being in hand 13 times with his score on 13, Jolly lost the match and England didn't win another.

All-in-all, Jolly was — and still is — the player with the greatest potential to cash in on open badminton. A more naturally-talented player than any other Briton of his time, he has both the flair and the magnetism to draw the crowds. He also has the approach of a winner, a real winner: 'England's men have been told for too long that they can't compete with the best in the world. People expect us to lose. That's not for me. All the big-name foreign players are only people; they can be beaten.' His determination is tremendous, but his temperament has often let him down, caused him to blow his chances and even to throw them away. For that he is often roundly condemned, but the tempestuous young man's critics should remember it is that same temperament that sometimes fires his superb victories.

Jolly's annoyance at not being part of the Masters at the Albert Hall was understandable: everybody with ambition would have liked to be in it, and clearly it was immensely important for Gillian Gilks. Unfortunately it had to be preceded by a two-week tour of Malaysia. When she was asked in the Spring to be available for this, it was due to take place in early August, but by the time the invitations officially arrived the date had moved on: the team were now not going to fly out until August 27th, and they would not be back until September 14th. The Masters was going to start on the 19th, and Gillian, to whom acclimatisation and preparation time is of high importance, was instantly worried that she wasn't going to have enough of either. She asked if she could withdraw; the chairman of selectors let it be known that if she did not play in Malaysia, she would not play at the Albert Hall. She went to Malaysia, where they had to play in a tournament the day after they arrived. Talbot, Jolly and Andy Goode lost in the third round, Stevens in the fourth; Karen Bridge and Barbara Sutton lost in the second round, Gilks, Perry and Webster in the quarter-finals — Gillian in straight games to a 20-year-old Indonesian, Tjan So Goan. Two weeks and 7,000 jet-miles later, they were trying to make glorious history in the Albert Hall.

That magnificent old building had often enough proved itself to be a great arena for sport, but for badminton it was something new. It was also something special, which is just what the game needed for this historic occasion. There is a feeling of excitement for the spectator as he takes his seat in the Albert Hall that can never arise in the mundane cavern of Wembley, and the BAE were absolutely right to take the plunge into that splendid unknown. It had everything going for it, but it also had drift, majestic drift. The odd thing was that the tournament director, Tommy Marrs, had been warned about it. In his own words, someone from the BBC (well accustomed to stringing lights and mikes across those vast aerial wastes) had suggested that 'sufficient air turbulence existed below that famous dome to frighten off helicopters.' Accordingly, he and Nick Budibent, the BAE Development and Publicity Officer, took rackets and shuttles into the hall one January morning to test the conditions. 'Fortunately our worst fears were not realised,' said Marrs, 'and as Mark Twain might have said, the rumour about the hall was exaggerated.' You could have fooled the players the following September, when high shuttles were dropping in most irregular parabolas. It may have mattered little to the crowds, but by all accounts it was hell on court.

The Friends' Provident Life Office were the sponsors of this first tournament of open badminton, for which the total prize money was £20,700 — equally divided, tennis players were interested to note, between men and women. The previous maximum prize for singles winners (£100) was guaranteed to each member of the doubles team that finished bottom of their group; a singles player who didn't win one game in the tournament, which was Nora Perry's unhappy record, still took home £250. It was enough to attract any badminton player seeking either money or glory, but a major disappointment surrounded the occasion. First and most obviously, only five of the 50 members of the Badminton Players' Association had signed forms to indicate that they were licensed players — the top Britons, Talbot, Stevens, Gilks, Perry and Webster. That meant, theoretically, that all the other players, including the Scandinavians, were still eligible for the Commonwealth Games (and the Olympics, if they ever happened); and that, while all the prize money had to be paid first to the national associations, it could only be passed on in full to those licensed British players. The others were still only entitled to their £100 maximum. There was, of course, nothing to stop them receiving other money in training grants, or expenses, or indeed in pension funds. The second disappointment was that the Friends' Provident Masters, while skimming the cream off the rest of the world, had not attracted either Indonesians or Malaysians, and nobody could pretend that the best badminton players in the world were in the Albert Hall while the Indonesians, at least, were absent.

But overall, despite those absences, it wasn't a bad do. The two groups of men were Delfs, Frost Hansen, Stevens and Zeniya; Kihlstrom, Padukone, Pri and Talbot. For the women, Perry faced Koppen, Yuki and Tokuda (no wonder she didn't win a game), and Gilks had Webster, Kondo and Carter. Out of those pools, Koppen and Gilks emerged undefeated, and Frost Hansen and Padukone, and none of them had lost a single game. The men's and women's doubles were each in one group of four pairs, the top two of which went through to the final; Kihlstrom and Froman of Sweden against Stevens and Tredgett, Yonekura and Tokuda of Japan against Perry and Webster. The Saturday afternoon of the finals was a marvellously atmospheric occasion, and not just because of the money at stake. No other venue in Britain, however worthy, could have contributed so fully to the excitement, despite the British disappointments.

Lene Koppen was by then Mrs Ropke, but it was not until the last day that the British Press acceded to her request (or perhaps understood it) that she wished to go on playing under her maiden name. By any name, she controlled Mrs Gilks, who stormed off to a 5–1 lead and had game point at 10–8, but lost 12–10, 11–4. Gillian was, as she later admitted, quite unable to compensate in the second game for the wild variation in conditions between the two ends of the court, caused by the almost farcical degree of drift. Lene Koppen, who has ever been the steadier player, made her adjustments with admirable lack of concern to earn her association £3,000. Prakash Padukone was not much troubled either, and the Swedish men's pair beat the Britons in two games; but the women's doubles was a tremendous match and brought victory to the comparatively newly-formed home team of Mrs Perry and Miss Webster, who in the pool had lost to the Japanese. What was most important for badminton was not the results, but the fact that the tournament had happened at all. The BAE had shown a strong hand, by planning the tournament and finding a sponsor even before the IBF had given the go-ahead to open badminton. Only the British players had declared their intention to go for money, and if the professional game was to succeed, it needed more bold associations and more bold players. Above all, it needed more highly-sponsored tournaments (which were to remain under the control of the IBF to the extent that the organisers had to apply for permission to stage them). In the programme for the Friends' Provident, IBF vice-president Craig Reedie quite excellently summed up the uncertain situation as it then stood:

> 'Those who are most likely to benefit must appreciate that the commercial return to them, as players, will demand from them a much more disciplined approach to the game. Once committed to playing in a tournament they must compete and excuses, ranging from sore feet to fog on the motorway, will not wash. They must also be prepared for more travel and the expense of living abroad. Top stars from England are now as commercially attractive in Denmark as they are here, which might mean a new order of priorities for both the player and the game in England.

> The new receipts must also be shared equitably. Nobody will grudge attractive prizes for players, but the promoting national organisation must be allowed its profit — even if that is mainly in public relations. The IBF will charge for its sanction and apply the income received from sanction fees to the development of the international game, development for all countries and for all interests. It will take some time to measure the impact of the new legislation and to see what effect the money has — or even if there is as much money as some would have us believe.'

It would be interesting to see, he concluded, if badminton could move from the most pleasant of indoor games to a mass participant sport and a glamorous television spectacle, while at the same time continuing to attract as its players the nicest of people. Perhaps there has not been enough time yet for those questions to be answered properly. The players are still there, most of them, but the movement has been disappointingly slow. Dreams of early glory faded fast.

14 Cutting loose

Nightmares seldom come in more horrible shape than did that badminton season of 1979–80 for Gillian Gilks. In the three months to the end of November, having lost to Lene Koppen in the Masters final, she lost the English Invitation singles final to Karen Bridge, the Bells Highland championship final to Nora Perry, an international against Denmark to Lene Koppen, the Northern final to Karen Bridge, and the Randers Open final in Denmark to Verawaty. In January she lost to Koppen again in Copenhagen and in March — the sweating climax in which you usually wake up screaming — she was put out in the first round of the All-England by a Danish schoolgirl, Kirsten Larsen. By then even her enemies were beginning to feel sympathetic. She only played three other tournaments in the whole season, and those she won: a Laing Grand Prix event at Farnborough in which she beat Nora Perry; the English Nationals, which she took for the seventh time, demolishing Jane Webster in the final; and the Essex Open, in which she beat Karen Bridge. For a woman unaccustomed ever to losing to a domestic player, it was enough to destroy her. Remember, she had never before been beaten by either Bridge or Perry.

Even the doubles didn't exactly go according to plan. That side of life had started with a slap in the face when Mrs Gilks was not nominated for the 1979 Masters. To be fair, she had rather offered the cheek: invited to partner Mrs Perry, she told the selectors she wanted to play with Miss Webster, with whom she would later be defending their National title. They spiked her guns by pairing Perry and Webster, and Mrs Gilks was not even asked to make up one of the two scratch pairs who completed the group. She did partner Miss Webster in the Highland (lost to Perry and Karen Puttick), the Laing (lost to Puttick and Karen Bridge), the Northern (won) and the Nationals (lost to Perry and Puttick). In November 1979 (before the Nationals) a partnership began that both in practice and principle gladdened the heart of English badminton: Perry and Gilks played together again, the first time for many years, and won the Randers Open in Denmark. In the final they fairly comfortably beat the current All-England champions, Verawaty and Wigoeno, and there was little doubt that in these two brilliant doubles players, England had a partnership that, at least in theory, was almost unbeatable. Ahead of them, between March and May, lay the All-England, European and World championships. Perhaps just at the right time for Mrs Gilks, whose singles batteries were running down, a life-saving doubles team had been formed. 'The new pair seem ideally suited,' wrote *The Times*, 'with the necessary different skills and personalities to complement each other to perfection.' Was everything, once more and at last, going to be all right again? It was not. Only ten days after winning the National Singles, Gillian Gilks was again at war with the Badminton Association.

The first the world at large knew of it was when the BAE published, on December 19th, the names of the ten men and ten women who were to form the training squad for the European and World championships. Mrs Gilks had been left out. According to a BAE statement, this was because of her unwillingness to confirm her availability for the European championships and her insistence on travelling separately to the World championships in Jakarta. 'It is felt that these two factors are not conducive to the building of team spirit and unfair to other players if additional costs are to be involved which may result in a fewer number of players being sent,' ran their turgid prose. Neither Mrs Gilks nor Mike Goodwin knew of the decision until it was published, though they had been called to a meeting with some of the selectors (and the BAE's new chief executive, former Air Vice-Marshal and rugby referee 'Larry' Lamb) while the Nationals were on.

Gillian Gilks' recollection of the outcome of that meeting was that she and Mike Goodwin told the BAE representatives that they had made satisfactory arrangements that enabled them both to go to Bali to acclimatize before joining the English team in Jakarta for the World championship, and that there was no question of extra expense for this operation falling on the Association. They had not finalised their personal arrangements for the European championships, for which Gillian was looking for some kind of similar sponsorship to cover Goodwin's presence there — which she regarded as extremely important if she were to produce her best performance. When the composition of the squad was published, she asked for another meeting with John Havers and company, at which the BAE made it immediately clear that they were not prepared to compromise. They insisted that Gillian would not be allowed to leave early for the World championships and would have to travel from London with the rest of the team if she wanted to compete at all. Faced with such an ultimatum, she capitulated and agreed to make herself available for selection.

Mrs Gilks was surprised to receive, a couple of days later, a letter from Larry Lamb asking for the signatures of both Gillian and Goodwin, confirming their agreement to the terms contained in the letter. These were, said Gillian, less flexible than those agreed at the meeting and required her to be available to play in all events at the European championships — a condition that, she said, had not been mentioned at the meeting. It meant, or could have meant, that she could be called on for singles and doubles in all the rubbers of the European team championships, to be followed as usual by the individual championships; which were to be followed a month later by the World championship in Indonesia. It was more than Mrs Gilks

The world had a glimpse of what could have been its greatest-ever women's doubles team when Gillian Gilks and Nora Perry won the All-England title in 1980

The tall Danish schoolgirl, Kirsten Larsen (left), *who put Gillian out of the 1980 All-England in the first round, was later extinguished by little Lene Koppen. Ms Koppen went on to win the title for the second successive year and received the trophy from Britain's Minister for Sport, Hector Monro*

thought she should be prepared to guarantee, and indeed it had been a specific plea at their meeting that she should not be put under such pressure. Nevertheless, on January 22nd, 1980, the BAE announced that all the outstanding problems between the two parties had now been resolved, and Mrs Gilks had been added to the squad for both forthcoming championships. Having said that she had earlier been 'uncooperative' over the travelling arrangements, John Havers now told the Press: 'The meeting between us was a victory for good sense. We explained our problem over the travelling issue and she and her coach began to see it would be better to be part and parcel of the team. I hope this will be the end of all the problems between Mrs Gilks and the Badminton Association.' Oh dear, oh Lord, so did we all! But new problems were creeping up behind her.

Only ten days later *The Times* came up with a story that Mrs Gilks had parted company with her coach, and without his guidance she was seriously considering retirement. According to Goodwin, the report continued, he had been led to believe that he must keep a low profile if he were to fulfil his ambition of progressing from county coach to national coach. John Woolhouse, chairman of the BAE coaching committee, admitted that he had told Goodwin in the past that 'he was not doing his own case any good by being associated with someone so constantly at odds with the establishment as Mrs Gilks.' (Other establishment figures, of course, were frequently suggesting to Mrs Gilks that she was not doing her case any good by tying herself so firmly to Mr Goodwin.)

Goodwin's understanding of that 'low profile' business was this: that if he kept his nose clean and didn't upset anybody, he would get his national badge. He had been at pains to do just that, advising Gillian to give in to the BAE requirements over the World and European championships and generally being careful to toe the line. Just the same, he didn't get the badge. This, together with the knowledge that Gillian was not going to have what he reckoned was the right preparation nor the right advice for the championships, was enough to push him into what was perhaps a rather petulant decision: he wouldn't coach her any more. That in turn led Gillian to say that if he wasn't coaching her, she probably wouldn't carry on after the All-England, which was only six weeks away. 'I thought,' Gillian said later, 'that if we were going to go to Jakarta late and I wouldn't be able to acclimatize properly and my coach wasn't going to be there anyway and the captain was someone I didn't get on with at all, there was no point in going. That was really the turning point.'

When the England team for the two great championships was announced on March 2nd (a month after *The Times* story), Mrs Gilks was not in it — finally and absolutely not in it. She confirmed to the Press Association: 'I have personal reasons for not wanting to go. It was my choice and it's true to say I am now thinking about retiring.' Retiring, she meant to say, from team events; that's what she told the selectors and this is what she told me: 'I've had enough. I'd rather play what I like and enjoy it than go on with all this hassle. I'm cutting loose. If I want to play good badminton, I have to get rid of the hassle. I finally snapped and said I'm not going to do it and I've been far happier since. Everything is much clearer now. I don't have to doff my cap to anybody and nobody else is pulling my strings.' She had persuaded Goodwin, meanwhile, to carry on as her coach. She won the Essex Open, beating Karen Bridge, and she and Nora Perry won both the Essex and the Danish Open, and that took her to the All-England — for the seventeenth time.

Just as there will never be another tournament quite like Wimbledon, so the All-England can never quite be equalled, whatever status and prize money is accumulated by other championships. It never ceases to surprise me that the preliminaries to play are so chaotic. The competitors are not allowed to play in the arena at Wembley until one hour before the tournament begins. Drop in early that first afternoon and you will see more than a hundred of the greatest badminton players in the world rushing for the courts when the moment comes, all desperate to get a feel of the floor and the atmosphere and the temperature — and the drift. There is no allocation of courts for practice, no time limit, seemingly no organisation — just first come, first to serve. Not only are the seven courts filled with players, but the space between the courts too, with shuttles looping over the high umpires' chairs. For most players, the day is planned around food: Gillian ate a good meal in mid-morning, and as she was not due on court till about 3.15, had time for a light snack after knocking-up. The previous day she went to the pictures in the afternoon, in the hope that it would help her to relax, and had a big meal fairly early in the evening. The first day's play is always heavy, and the fact that in 1980 the tournament was to go on a day longer than usual, till Sunday, did not make that any better, though it relieved the situation later in the week. In that first day Gillian was expecting to play two singles and three mixed doubles, probably not finishing until midnight. By the time she was back home in Barnet and relaxed enough to sleep, it would be well into the morning.

The women's seeding this time put Lene Koppen and Wiharjo Verawaty at the opposite ends of the draw, with Gillian and Yoshiko Yonekura scheduled to meet them in the semi-finals. In the quarter-finals, Saori Kondo was the expected opponent, so there was plenty of trouble ahead for the only English player with any chance of a singles title. In the first round Mrs Gilks was drawn against an 18-year-old Danish girl, Kirsten Larsen, unknown to most of the English public, but just the same, she was the European junior champion. An unpredictable girl, said Gillian: 'In January she went out to Japan and beat both Kondo and Verawaty, then she came back to Denmark and lost her under-18 event.' Gillian was in high spirits on the eve of the tournament, strong (she had, for the first time included weightlifting in her training), mentally sharp and, at last, confident: 'Ever since the start of the season I've been having more downs than ups,' she said, 'both in playing and training, but now it's starting to go the other way.'

The direction was reversed the next day. For Mrs Gilks, as Richard Streeton put it in *The Times*, 'the match represented 23 minutes of humiliation and agony. She has not often had to experience the cruel levelling factor that sport can be nor the frustrations that the passage of the years can bring. At 29, Mrs Gilks was dreadfully slow about the court in contrast to her young opponent and this, coupled with her inability to find length or accuracy, left her floundering.' The tall young Dane (even taller than Gillian) had never played at Wembley before, but she showed no sign of nerves. Miss Larsen opened the serving and ran to 8–0 before the former champion got the shuttle in her hands. Even then Gillian did not win a point. Larsen had reached 10–0, game point, before she conceded one, and she took the first game 11–4. Gilks led 3–0 in the second, trailed 3–6, reached 6–6 and didn't score again. It was uncanny.

Afterwards Mrs Gilks offered no excuses: 'I tried everything and she countered everything. It was unbelievable. Nothing was working, and there's nothing worse than being in a tight corner, with the match running away from you, and every shot you try just doesn't work. I didn't have any control. Now I'm just empty, terribly disappointed.' So it was Miss Larsen who had two singles matches that first day, and in the second she destroyed an English teenager, Nicola Bewley. The next day she beat an Indian, Ami Ghia, and in the quarter-final on Friday she faced another seed, former finalist Saori Kondo. Larsen won 11–5, 11–9, thus reaching the semi-final against Lene Koppen without having lost a game. Alas, against her brilliant compatriot she won not a single point. She was ground into the boards by a queen who showed no hint of mercy — a defeat that was probably assured in Miss Larsen's mind before they ever reached the court.

In the mixed Mrs Gilks, playing with Svend Pri, won only two matches before falling to Dave Eddy and Barbara Sutton, but the women's doubles went splendidly. She and Nora Perry conceded only 12 points in their first three matches before beating Kondo and Takada 15–5, 15–1 in the semi. The English pair faced Tokuda and Yonekura in the final, and after a slightly disjointed first game produced a triumph of double craft to take the title. It was the third time, with different partners, that Gillian had won the All-England doubles and it was overall her ninth title of those championships. With no great delicacy of timing, the England selectors then announced publicly that after 15 months of attempted conciliation, they were now abandoning all attempts to bring Mrs Gilks back into the fold.

'I enjoyed those doubles,' said Gillian. 'I've really always enjoyed playing doubles more than singles. I was so nervous inside before an important singles match that if it were not converted into proper energy it could get the better of me. The trouble is you can't prove yourself the best in the world unless you play singles, there's no arguing with that.'

So the England team went off to Groningen and Jakarta in the Spring of 1980, and Gillian Gilks went on holiday. She went to Antigua for a fortnight in the sun with two badminton players, Barbara Beckett, the Irish number one, and Paula Kilvington. The former English junior champion was then ranked number five in England, but was not even named as the reserve to the five women in the team for the World and European championships. Reckoning that she had not had a fair deal from the selectors, Miss Kilvington announced at the beginning of April that, though she desperately wanted to play for England again, she would not do so until selection was based more on results in open tournaments than on those in invitation events with restricted entries. Not surprisingly, both Miss Kilvington and Barbara Beckett threw in their lot with Gillian and Mike Goodwin in the summer, and a highly independent, somewhat rebellious badminton training camp was set up. The fact that they were some way outside the walls of the establishment did not harm their badminton, but one major problem had to be faced: since they were never going to be official nominees of the BAE for any tournament, and since they could not be sure that invitations addressed to them through the BAE would ever be passed on, they had to make direct contact with those organisers in whose tournaments they wanted to play — particularly the overseas ones. The principle on which the BAE worked was quite clear, and they were not ashamed of it: whatever any overseas organiser was prepared to offer English players in the way of fares, expenses, hospitality and prize money was going to go to English players who were available to play for England and not to the renegades. In an amateur sport, it would be hard to quarrel with that system; but badminton was now a game in which the top players earned a full-time living and all manner of unpleasant complexities arose when a governing body decided to choke a player's right to earn her living.

The most critical example of the problems Mrs Gilks was going to have to face as she pursued her private badminton battles came with the second of the high-prestige, high prize money Friends' Provident Masters tournaments at the Albert Hall at the beginning of the 1980–81 season. The lady had, you may remember, been the runner-up to Lene Koppen the previous year, and was still outstandingly the best player in England, as well as being officially ranked number one in the country. And yet, as we all could have anticipated, she was not invited to compete for a share of the £7,500 available for the women's singles. Eight women were invited and one of them was England's number two, Karen Bridge. As the BAE had been sticking to the line that Gillian Gilks had retired after the All-England, her solicitors began writing to the Association in the spring to point out that she had not retired from individual competition, and was available for the Friends' Provident. For one reason or another, said Mrs Gilks, that didn't do any good: the official line was that the invitations had all gone out and been accepted, and it was not likely that anyone would drop out to accommodate her. Teeth were gnashed in Barnet, but what more could be done? Then, the week before the tournament, Hiroe Yuki had to withdraw. Her place would be taken, the BAE announced, by Jane Webster. Now, at that time Miss Webster (who was already playing in the tournament as Nora Perry's partner) was ranked number four in England and had never beaten Gillian Gilks. But she was, the Association pointed out, the official reserve; and besides, Mrs Gilks' international results did not justify inviting her to compete in the Masters — presumably a reference to her first-round defeat in the All-England, since she had reached the final of every other international competition she had entered the previous season. It was like being hit in the face with a wet fish; the ultimate affront, the final humiliation.

So the Friends' Provident went on without Britain's finest singles player — and perhaps the saddest blow was that, so far as independent observers at the scene could establish, there was no longer much sympathy for Mrs Gilks even from the players. Interviewed on radio, Ray Stevens did little more than repeat the official BAE line about Gillian's results not justifying her selection. 'My results are so much better than Ray's, I don't know how he has the gall to say it,' responded Gillian. 'He hardly ever gets to the singles finals of international events. I do think that's unfair.' It was another example, she said, of the way the BAE had brain-washed the other players. Fortunately, Mrs Gilks did not hear a female member of the England team say that she would have walked out if Gillian had played at the Albert Hall. In the end it was, once again, a splendidly-mounted tournament that attracted too few people in mid-week but a great crowd at the end. The English representatives no doubt did their best, but it wasn't greatly impressive. Stevens, Bridge and Webster all managed only one win each in their singles groups; neither Stevens and Mike Tredgett nor Tredgett and Nora Perry made the final of the men's and mixed doubles (Tredgett and Perry were, crucially, beaten in two games by little Karen Chapman and Scotland's big Billy Gilliland); and the women's pair, Perry and Webster, lost a fine final to Tokuda and Yonekura. Koppen and Swie King took away another £3,000 each, Koppen playing with such assurance and poise it seemed possible that even in the badminton hell-hole of Indonesia, the Indonesians would not upset her. But they did. Koppen went out to Ivana in that semi-final, who lost to Verawaty. Indonesians indeed took every World title in Jakarta except the women's doubles, quite superbly won by Perry and Webster.

They had by then won the European title too, as Tredgett and Perry had the mixed. No other English contenders at Groningen got further than the semis, which was extremely disappointing. Little wonder, perhaps, that in the summer the Badminton Association once again changed their managerial and selectorial system: with the Association moving their headquarters to Milton Keynes, selector Ciro Ciniglio was appointed full-time team and coaching manager, and Paul Whetnall was named coach for the Uber Cup. The Uber squad was announced too. Eight women, but not, of course, Gillian Gilks.

15 The best of British

It is not easy to grasp just how far across the modern history of badminton Gillian Gilks' career reaches. She was playing for England when Karen Bridge was only six years old, and her doubles partner then was a lady who had been playing ever since the war. Gillian was playing in the All-England senior championships before Sally Leadbeater (England's reserve in the 1980 world championship) was old enough to walk. And even now Gillian is only 30, six years younger than Judy Hashman was when she last played for England.

Gillian tip-toed into senior badminton soon after the annual English Nationals had been launched and the domestic crown was being disputed between Ursula Smith and Angela Bairstow — as it was for some years to come. Judy Hashman was still an American then, and the year Gillian first played in the All-England senior (1965) was the year Mrs Hashman's unrivalled run of wins was interrupted by Miss Smith. 'No question that Judy was the greatest player of her time,' said Gillian. 'Though I saw her winning her last All-Englands, I never saw her play at her best. By the time she came over here and played for England, her age had made it more difficult for her to maintain attacking play and she had begun to lift and defend a bit too much. Angela never won the All-England, but because Ursula left the country and went to South Africa it was Angie, most of the time, that I had to beat to get to the top. They were both strongly-built, very determined girls — I must have looked like a ghost beside them then — but Ursula was not quite so outgoing as Angie. Ursula had an extraordinary service, very high and produced almost automatically, almost like a serving machine. You knew exactly where it was going, but it still wasn't particularly easy to take. Half the time you were wondering if it was going to hit the ceiling.'

Two others close to young Gillian at the time were her contemporary Jane Colman and the much older player, Iris Rogers — both Wimbledon and Surrey players, both doubles partners of hers. 'In the very early days, Jane seemed to have more talent than I did, and more strokes, but she wasn't exactly single-minded about badminton. She took up with fellas pretty early — she was engaged at 16 — and lost interest a bit at the time when she needed to apply herself very thoroughly if she wanted to make it to the top. Iris was marvellous. Probably not the greatest of singles

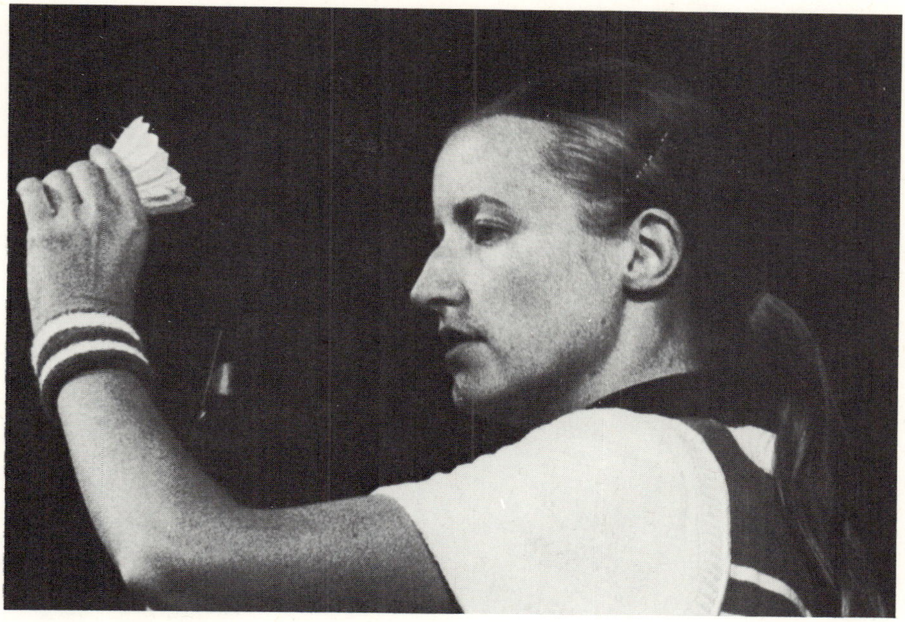

The most startling physical transformation ever seen in sport: Gillian Gilks before and after plastic surgery

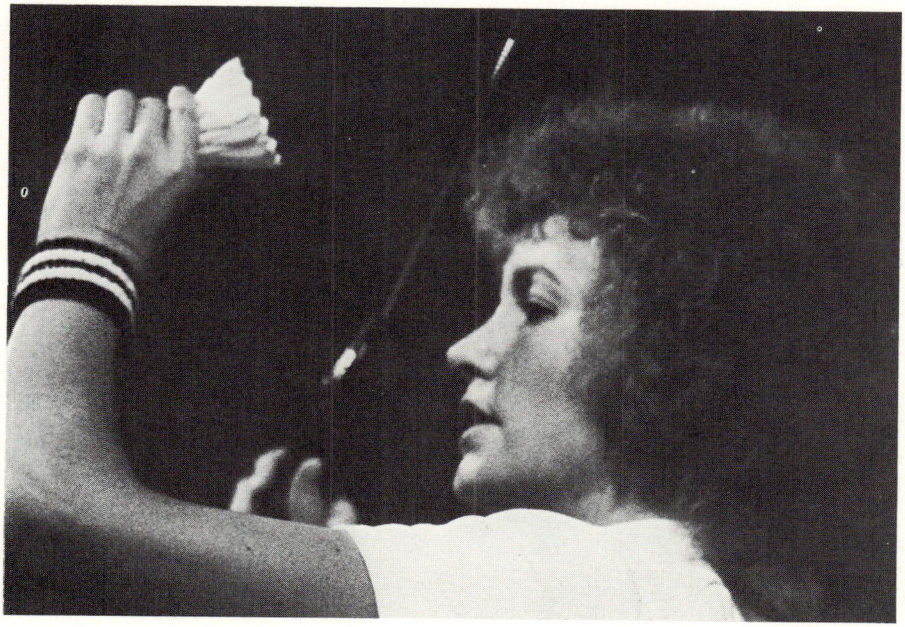

New face, new hair style, same trophy: Gillian wins the English Nationals in 1980 for the eighth time

players — though again I never saw her at her best — but a marvellous person to have for your doubles partner when you were young and tentative. She was very strong and dependable, with a wonderful temperament. It was from her that I learned to accept a bad line call without letting it affect my play, and if you can learn that while you're young it's worth a lot of points.'

The two men at the top of the English singles game at that time were Colin Beacom and Roger Mills, who could scarcely have been further apart in style. Beacom was a big player with a big wind-up and a big swing, a man who lived by clearing and smashing. Mills was small and accurate, a very precise player, a man of drives, flicks and placings. It was with him that Gillian won her first All-England title, the mixed in 1969. 'On the whole the partnership worked very well. He didn't have a particularly strong smash from the back of the court, so I had to make sure I finished it off at the net. That brought me on tremendously. The partnership didn't continue as long as it might because he had business commitments that prevented his going abroad sometimes.' A forceful, forthright personality, Mills became the national coach and was dismissed when the BAE thought that his contract with a manufacturer conflicted with his position. The parting was rather bitter and an industrial tribunal was brought in to settle their differences. Even now Mills is not slow to stick thorns in the Association's side when he thinks they need them, which perhaps is no bad thing.

Mills and Beacom were chased from the domestic throne by Ray Sharp and Paul Whetnall, of whom Whetnall had much the longer and the more successful badminton career. The chasing occurred neatly during the English Nationals of 1967, when the two younger men beat the two older in the semi-finals, and never again let them in to a major title. Sharp reached his peak ahead of Whetnall, but when Whetnall got there he was almost impossible to dislodge. As a leading junior, he looked like an angelic choirboy, with his fair, curly hair and expression of juvenile innocence. Under Jake Downey's training, he became extremely fast on the court and advanced well ahead of his English rivals. He was also well ahead of them in the matter of securing the attention of Sue Pound, an elegant young Kent player who won her first international cap in the same 1966 match against Scotland as that which blooded Gillian Gilks. Sue, who developed one of the world's great doubles partnerships with Margaret Boxall, had a slow and easy style that she was often able to impose on a singles match. When she did, there were few to beat her. The Whetnalls were quite unable to strike up a satisfactory partnership on the court, where Paul and Miss Boxall were an extremely effective pair — frequently challenged in finals by either Sue and Tony Jordan or Gillian and Roger Mills. The two Whetnalls twice left the amateur game, first as part of the John Beirne professional circus and later when Paul went to Canada as the national coach.

Whetnall was probably at his peak then, and the man who replaced him at the summit of English singles play was the splendid Derek Talbot of Newcastle — not renowned as a breeding ground of badminton champions. He played for his county at 16, but had to come to live in London before he was picked for England. Once in, he stayed and held top place in the rankings till he was 32. A magnificent retriever, he could have remained an outstanding doubles player for years beyond that, but in 1980 retired from the competitive game to concentrate on his own sports goods business. His partnerships with Elliot Stuart and with Gillian Gilks deserve to remain long honoured in the history of British badminton. Apart from his Commonwealth and European gold medals, he three times won the All-England mixed with Gillian. Like Sharp and Whetnall, and like Ray Stevens who succeeded him, Talbot reached the highest level it was possible to reach in Britain. To improve their game, they would have had to live abroad, or at least to spend much of the season in either Denmark or Indonesia. British women often figure among the very best players in the world, but no British man has been a leading singles contender in the past 40 years. The women can go on improving because they can practise against men who are stronger and faster than they are; our top men can never do that. Nor, until recently, could they afford to devote themselves entirely to the game in the way that the Danes and the Far Eastern players could. And even now that international prize money is high enough to satisfy the hungriest, it does not do much good to the Britons, who at their most optimistic know they still have no chance of beating the best of the rest of the world. Kevin Jolly believes he has, and on the basis of his talent and determination at an early age he certainly has a better chance than any other Englishman since the war; but it will be surprising if he manages to achieve his dreams without much more travel than the British are used to — and without, incidentally, a radical adjustment of the BAE's control mechanism.

Almost all the leading Danish players live (and work, when necessary) around Copenhagen, where there is a very well-organised and competitive club system. National practice is easy and frequent (in England it is rare), and that little nation goes on producing champions at badminton — though seldom in any other sport. After the great Erland Kops came Svend (Andersen) Pri, who took a year off work in order to train to win the All-England. He did, beating Rudy Hartono in 1975. When his severe hamstring injury took him out of the game, there was Flemming Delfs to win the European, All-England and World titles; and constantly breathing fire down his neck is Morton Frost Hansen — the potential champions just keep coming. That they keep coming in Indonesia too is less surprising: the game is unashamedly part of their way of life, and a way that is made very smooth for those with the necessary talent. They have the advantage too that most Europeans find it very difficult to play at their best in the tropical heat and humidity of that country. Champions will not survive unless they can win in Indonesia.

That means beating players like Hartono and Swie King on their own ground, a truly Herculean task. It means subduing Wiharjo Verawaty at 90 degrees Fahrenheit, and finding a way of destroying doubles partnerships like Verawaty and Wigoeno, Chandra and Christian, Tjun Tjun and Wahjudi, Christian and Wigoeno when the western body seems to be dissolving into its shoes. The presence of those

Gillian opened the 1980–81 season by winning the Welsh Open singles at Cardiff, and the doubles with her new partner, Paula Kilvington

Barely recognisable until she began to play, the new Gillian Gilks faces the future happier and with more confidence

two brilliant men's doubles pairs (who have only failed to win the All-England title once in the past eight years) has meant that Hartono and Swie King have not had to bother themselves with playing doubles seriously. It is one of the rotten elements of the English system that almost all its outstanding players, of either sex, are expected to bang in on all fronts at once, meaning that they are frequently tied to the arena for 12 hours at a time. That is not the way to succeed, and the sooner we realise it the better. Nora Perry got the message, and pulled out of top singles play; Gillian Gilks herself withdrew from the 1981 All-England singles; if Karen Bridge and Kevin Jolly are to fulfil their promise, they should abandon the doubles game at times of greatest stress.

Mike Tredgett did exactly the right thing, too. A few years ago he was one of the top four singles players in England, but it was clear he was never going to make it right to the top. He was always killing himself in the semi-finals trying in vain to beat Talbot or Stevens, and then he would suffer with muscle trouble in the doubles. It was clear when he was a junior that he was going to be a very good doubles player, and in the end that's what he went for. Like his partner Nora Perry, he stopped contesting the major singles titles. When a man enters all three events and makes it to the finals, he is in for a very hard time. Not only are men on court longer than the women, but they meet comparatively stronger opposition and often have to play more rounds, because of the larger entry. All bounce and muscle, little Tredgett and big Perry were, at their peak, the best mixed pair in the world and probably the most popular. When they lost their Friends' Provident Masters title at the Albert Hall in 1980, Tredgett was noticeably slower than he had been — unlike all the other leading players in the game, he had full-time job responsibilities.

Gillian Gilks reckons that it may still just be possible for a young player who is heading for England selection to do so and hold down a job, but that is becoming increasingly difficult. It would take a highly-organised youngster to do it. You would have to live within reach of the big domestic tournaments, play in them two out of three weekends and get results — as well as spending a lot of time practising. If you live in Cornwall, you would have to leave it and go to share a convenient flat with some others who were going to dedicate themselves to the game. Then you could travel together, be coached together and practise together. Between you, you would have at the beginning of the season to decide what tournaments you were going to enter. That decision would have to be taken not only on the basis of location, but of standard of play. Are you going to go to lesser tournaments and do really well, or the better ones and improve your play against others of a higher standard? If your name is not known, there is no guarantee anyway that you would be accepted for a big tournament, but some of them do hold qualifying rounds which would give you the chance of making it. Unfortunately these qualifying rounds are held before the main tournament begins, either earlier in the day or on an evening in mid-week — very difficult for people who are working.

It is probably easier to survive at this stage in your badminton life on the dole rather than in work, and some have made it with no more help than that. Many, of course, have their parents to thank for supporting them up to the time when their results have produced sufficient interest for an equipment manufacturer to offer a little sponsorship — providing clothes and rackets, paying tournament entry fees, meeting travel costs; no more than that for a start, but it does give the young player extra incentive. It is not entirely a philanthropic act by the manufacturer. He will be looking, and always is, for tomorrow's top players. He wants his name to be the one on the All-England final court, and not that of his rival. But even a little sponsorship seems a long way ahead to an aspiring schoolboy or girl. How are they going to get that far?

Gillian Gilks played for England when she was still at school, but she was not playing badminton at school. Today the chances are that your talent and interest will have been discovered at school, and that you will move from school representative matches to county junior squad and matches. At the same time as the school commitments are going on, the youngster who is getting encouraging results will be keeping an eye on national age-group tournaments. Gillian's first national contest was in the All-England under-18 championships, at the age of 11. The next year under-15 championships began (she won them), and now there are under-any age you care to mention. What it all adds up to is that there are far more demands on a youngster now to play in events than there ever were 20 years ago. This may be all very well, but it leaves correspondingly less time for practice, and how do you groom your strokes and iron out your faults without practice? In a match, the tendency is to play safe, not to try risky shots or develop new strokes. But you will need those strokes if you are to improve, and the only way to acquire them is in practice. The person you are practising with does not have to be particularly good, but he needs patiently to feed you the right shuttles so that you can go on working on your backhand clear or the mid-court smash.

If you are outstandingly good at 13, the chances are that you will go on being good at all age groups. You might have a year or two levelling out, when your results are not so terrific, but you will almost certainly climb again. The discouraging time may come when you reach 18. There is often a huge gap between being an All-England junior semi-finalist and winning even one match in the senior tournament, and that is where a lot of youngsters used to fall out of the game. It is depressing for talented young players trying to break into the England squad, which is not very large, to find people like Talbot and Gilks who have been sitting there for 10 years and show no sign of going. Well, they are out of the squad now and a new generation is emerging — Goode, Scott, Leadbeater, Kilvington, Clark are all hammering on the door for a chance to follow Jolly and Bridge to the top. Not everybody begins early, by the way: Iris Rogers didn't play seriously until she was 16, and by 19 she was playing for England.

The talented and aspiring young player, of either sex, will probably be named for an English national training squad before he appears on the ranking list of the top 10 players. To reach either stage will almost certainly be the most exciting moment of his badminton life so far. He will have achieved it by carefully directing his talent and determination, under the guidance of his coach, to the area where it can do most good. It's no good to start the season with the fiery purpose of beating Karen Bridge or Kevin Jolly and that will show them. Pick off the players who are ranked above you one by one, starting with the least secure member of the squad. A victory over him will not be overlooked at headquarters; and when that has been achieved, go for the next one. It won't necessarily follow that the ranking list will instantly be changed, but when the selectors next meet, the facts will be there. The history of international success seems to suggest, says Mrs Gilks, that a player may peak early and reach his maximum potential by the time he is 20, or he may progress less spectacularly and win the All-England at 26. Either way, remember this: badminton is not like swimming, where you pass your best almost as soon as you reach it. It is not even like running, in which only one sprinter of either sex has ever won a gold medal in two Olympic Games. It is a sport in which dedication can lead to a long career at the top. By the time you are 30, you may have lost some speed, but your experience and your craft will have made you a very difficult player to beat. Look at Rudy Hartono. Look at Gillian Gilks.

Addendum: Badminton champions 1965–1980

World titles:

	Men's singles	*Women's singles*
1977	Flemming Delfs (Denmark)	Lene Koppen (Denmark)
1980	Rudy Hartono (Indonesia)	Wiharjo Verawaty (Indonesia)

	Men's doubles	*Women's doubles*	*Mixed doubles*
1977	Tjun Tjun & Wahjudi (Indonesia)	Toganoo & Ueno (Japan)	Skovgaard & Koppen (Denmark)
1980	Chandra & Christian (Indonesia)	Perry & Webster (England)	Christian & Wigoeno (Indonesia)

All-England titles:

	Men's singles	*Women's singles*
1965	Erland Kops (Denmark)	Ursula Smith (England)
1966	Tan Aik Huang (Malaysia)	Judy Hashman (USA)
1967	Erland Kops (Denmark)	Judy Hashman (USA)
1968	Rudy Hartono (Indonesia)	Eva Twedberg (Sweden)
1969	Rudy Hartono (Indonesia)	Hiroe Yuki (Japan)
1970	Rudy Hartono (Indonesia)	Etsuko Takenaka (Japan)
1971	Rudy Hartono (Indonesia)	Eva Twedberg (Sweden)
1972	Rudy Hartono (Indonesia)	Noriko Nakayama (Japan)
1973	Rudy Hartono (Indonesia)	Margaret Beck (England)
1974	Rudy Hartono (Indonesia)	Hiroe Yuki (Japan)
1975	Svend Pri (Denmark)	Hiroe Yuki (Japan)
1976	Rudy Hartono (Indonesia)	Gillian Gilks (England)
1977	Flemming Delfs (Denmark)	Hiroe Yuki (Japan)

1978	Liem Swie King (Indonesia)	Gillian Gilks (England)
1979	Liem Swie King (Indonesia)	Lene Koppen (Denmark)
1980	Prakash Padukone (India)	Lene Koppen (Denmark)

	Men's doubles	*Women's doubles*	*Mixed doubles*
1965	Boon Bee & Yee Khan (Malaysia)	Jorgensen & Strand (Denmark)	Kobbero & Strand (Denmark)
1966	Boon Bee & Yee Khan (Malaysia)	Hashman & Peard (USA/Ireland)	Kobbero & Strand (Denmark)
1967	Kops & Borch (Denmark)	Rietveld & Strand (Holland/Denmark)	Andersen & Strand (Denmark)
1968	Kops & Borch (Denmark)	Koestijah & Minarni (Indonesia)	Jordan & Pound (England)
1969	Kops & Borch (Denmark)	Boxall & Whetnall (England)	Mills & Perrin (England)
1970	Bacher & Peterzen (Denmark)	Boxall & Whetnall (England)	Walsoe & Hansen (Denmark)
1971	Boon Bee & Gunalan (Malaysia)	Takagi & Yuki (Japan)	Pri & Strand (Denmark)
1972	Chandra & Christian (Indonesia)	Aizawa & Takenaka (Japan)	Pri & Strand (Denmark)
1973	Chandra & Christian (Indonesia)	Aizawa & Takenaka (Japan)	Talbot & Gilks (England)
1974	Tjun Tjuh & Wahjudi (Indonesia)	Beck & Gilks (England)	Eddy & Whetnall (England)
1975	Tjun Tjun & Wahjudi (Indonesia)	Aizawa & Takenaka (Japan)	Stuart & Gardner (England)
1976	Froman & Kihlstrom (Sweden)	Gilks & Whetnall (England)	Talbot & Gilks (England)
1977	Tjun Tjun & Wahjudi (Indonesia)	Toganoo & Ueno (Japan)	Talbot & Gilks (England)
1978	Tjun Tjun & Wahjudi (Indonesia)	Takada & Tokuda (Japan)	Tredgett & Perry (England)
1979	Tjun Tjun & Wahjudi (Indonesia)	Verawaty & Wigoeno (Indonesia)	Christian & Wigoeno (Indonesia)
1980	Tjun Tjun & Wahjudi (Indonesia)	Gilks & Perry (England)	Tredgett & Perry (England)

European titles:

	Men's singles	*Women's singles*
1968	Sture Johnsson (Sweden)	Irmgard Latz (W. Germany)
1970	Sture Johnsson (Sweden)	Eva Twedberg (Sweden)

1972	Wolfgang Bochow (W. Germany)	Margaret Beck (England)
1974	Sture Johnsson (Sweden)	Gillian Gilks (England)
1976	Flemming Delfs (Denmark)	Gillian Gilks (England)
1978	Flemming Delfs (Denmark)	Lene Koppen (Denmark)
1980	Flemming Delfs (Denmark)	Liselotte Blumer (Switzerland)

	Men's doubles	*Women's doubles*	*Mixed doubles*	*Team*
1968	Eddy & Powell (England)	Boxall & Whetnall (England)	Jordan & Whetnall (England)	–
1970	Hansen & Walsoe (Denmark)	Boxall & Whetnall (England)	Eddy & Whetnall (England)	–
1972	Braun & Maywald (W. Germany)	Gilks & Hashman (England)	Talbot & Gilks (England)	England
1974	Braun & Maywald (W. Germany)	Beck & Gilks (England)	Talbot & Gilks (England)	England
1976	Stevens & Tredgett (England)	Gilks & Whetnall (England)	Talbot & Gilks (England)	Denmark
1978	Stevens & Tredgett (England)	Perry & Statt (England)	Tredgett & Perry (England)	England
1980	Karlsson & Nordin (Sweden)	Perry & Webster (England)	Tredgett & Perry (England)	Denmark

Commonwealth Games titles:

	Men's singles	*Women's singles*
1966	Tan Aik Huang (Malaysia)	Angela Bairstow (England)
1970	Jamie Paulson (Canada)	Margaret Beck (England)
1974	Punch Gunalan (Malaysia)	Gillian Gilks (England)
1978	Prakash Padukone (India)	Sylvia Ng (Malaysia)

	Men's doubles	*Women's doubles*
1966	Huang & Hoe (Malaysia)	Horton & Smith (England)
1970	Boon Bee & Gunalan (Malaysia)	Boxall & Whetnall (England)

1974	Stuart & Talbot (England)	Beck & Gilks (England)
1978	Stevens & Tredgett (England)	Perry & Statt (England)

Mixed doubles

1966	Mills & Bairstow (England)
1970	Talbot & Boxall (England)
1974	Talbot & Gilks (England)
1978	Tredgett & Perry (England)

English National titles:

	Men's singles	*Women's singles*
1965	Roger Mills	Ursula Smith
1966	Roger Mills	Ursula Smith
1967	Ray Sharp	Angela Bairstow
1968	Ray Sharp	Gillian Perrin
1969	Paul Whetnall	Gillian Perrin
1970	Derek Talbot	Gillian Gilks
1971	Derek Talbot	Margaret Beck
1972	Ray Stevens	Margaret Beck
1973	Derek Talbot	Margaret Beck
1974	Paul Whetnall	Margaret Beck
1975	Paul Whetnall	Gillian Gilks
1976	Ray Stevens	Margaret Lockwood
1977	Derek Talbot	Gillian Gilks
1978	Ray Stevens	Gillian Gilks

1979	Ray Stevens	Gillian Gilks	
1980	Ray Stevens	Gillian Gilks	

	Men's doubles	*Women's doubles*	*Mixed doubles*
1965	Beacom & Jordan	Bairstow & Barrand	Jordan & Charles
1966	Horton & Mills	Boxall & Pound	Horton & Horton
1967	Beacom & Jordan	Boxall & Pound	Mills & Perrin
1968	Eddy & Powell	Boxall & Whetnall	Mills & Perrin
1969	Jordan & Mills	Boxall & Whetnall	Whetnall & Boxall
1970	Stuart & Talbot	Beck & Rickard	Mills & Gilks
1971	Stuart & Talbot	Gilks & Hashman	Talbot & Gilks
1972	Stevens & Tredgett	Gilks & Hashman	Hunt & Gilks
1973	Stuart & Talbot	Gardner & Gilks	Talbot & Gilks
1974	Eddy & Sutton	Boxall & Whetnall	Talbot & Gilks
1975	Stevens & Tredgett	Gilks & Whetnall	Talbot & Gilks
1976	Stevens & Tredgett	Giles & Gilks	Tredgett & Gardner
1977	Stevens & Tredgett	Perry & Statt	Tredgett & Perry
1978	Stevens & Tredgett	Gilks & Webster	Tredgett & Perry
1979	Stevens & Tredgett	Perry & Puttick	Tredgett & Perry
1980	Stevens & Tredgett	Bridge & Sutton	Tredgett & Perry

Thomas Cup

1966–7	Malaysia
1969–70	Indonesia
1972–3	Indonesia
1975–6	Indonesia
1978–9	Indonesia

Uber Cup

1965–6	Japan
1968–9	Japan
1971–2	Japan
1974–5	Indonesia
1977–8	Japan

(Note changes of name: Miss Takenaka (Japan) became Mrs Toganoo; S. Andersen (Denmark) — Svend Pri; Miss Charles — Mrs Rickard; Miss Pound — Mrs Whetnall; Miss Perrin — Mrs Gilks; Miss Beck — Mrs Lockwood; Miss Gardner — Mrs Perry; Miss Giles — Sutton)